FROM SPECULATION TO REVELATION

The Difference Between Opinions and Facts Regarding God's Word

Bishop Donmaid Brooks

Copyright © 2013 by Bishop Donmaid Brooks
Los Angeles, California
All rights reserved
Printed and Bound in the United States of America

Published and Distributed by:
BD Brooks Publishing
Carson, California 90745
bishopdbrooks@gmail.com

Cover design by Jay De Vance III
First printing: January 2014
978-0-615-91272-1
Library of Congress Control Number is 20133922961
10987654321

Greek and Hebrew came from Strong Exhaustive Concordance

Scriptures taken from the New King James Version (N.K.J.)

No part of this book may be reproduced, stored in a retrieval system or transmitted in any form or by any means without the prior written permission of the publisher—except by a reviewer who may quote brief passages in a review to be printed in a newspaper, magazine or journal.

Acknowledgments

First off, I would like to thank my Lord and savior for the revelations that He has given me. As well as the grace He has shown me.

I would like to thank my mom, Margie Cox, for all her support, and love that she gave me. Thanks mom for the motivation, love, patience, hope and financial support that kept me going on. I love you, Mom, so much.

I would like to thank my managers, Timothy Morganfield and L-Tayna Madrie, for all the help they gave me, and for starting me off on this journey.

I would like to give a special thanks to Annette Jean Booker (R.I.P.) who was there to keep me focus on my mission. I love you Jean. May God bless your soul. I know you are in heaven, smiling and saying that you are proud of me.

I would like to thank my kids and family for always being there when things are not going well. I love all of you.

Special thanks to Rochelle Santiful for her encouragement and financial support.

I would like to thank Rosie Milligan, and the whole team that worked hard to bring my thoughts to paper. I would also like to thank my two brothers, Donja Brooks for being my protector when I needed someone to be there for me, and Donald Ray Brooks for showing us all how to be a man of integrity. I love you all and thank you, family, for all the psychological, emotional, and financial support that you have given me through the years. My God bless you all.

TABLE OF CONTENTS

About the Author 6

Chapter 1 9

Chapter 2 32

Chapter 3 54

Chapter 4 102

Chapter 5 119

About the Author

*W*ell, I know you may be wondering the history of how I was ordained a bishop. Well, let me tell you. I was ordained a bishop by the most looked upon people in the world…prison inmates. Yes! I was a convict. I have served time in nine different prisons. I can truly say that I was everything that is contradistinctive to the law and the Word of God. I grew up in the Compton/Los Angeles area of California. I started with Juvenile Hall. From there, I graduated to camp for being one of the most disobedient kids. Then I graduated from camp and earned my Bachelor's in Breaking the Law, taking things that did not belong to me. I thought that was really cool. So when I turned eighteen years old, I went to a popular school called LA County Jail. I did really well there because I made honor roll for fighting and starting riots. Afterwards, I enrolled into Chino State Prison. While there, I felt that I should get more education in stealing and breaking the law, but in a sneakier way so that I would not get caught. That did not work out so well, so I then enrolled into a better school called San Quentin State Prison where I earned my Master's Degree in lying, cheating, and fighting to show that I was down for whatever came my way. Well, that did not satisfy me enough, so I went to Chuckawalla Valley State Prison to earn my Ph.D. in everything there is to know about doing wrong. However, something happened in my last nine months of my three-year prison sentence. I cried out to God for answers, and God met me right in that prison cell and gave me something that I will never forget. From that day on, I began teaching people everything God has revealed to me. I've worked hard by living it, and preaching it to everyone that will listen. The people started coming to me from all denominational backgrounds, asking me all kinds of biblical questions. And thank God that I was able to answer all their questions. I was also able to help ministers and preachers to come to a better understanding of the Bible. Therefore, people began to call me Bishop Brooks. So there you have it. And NO! I have not been to seminary school, or any theology school, or college. The sad thing is I have not even graduated from high school. Unfortunately, I dropped out of school in the ninth grade and never returned. Now I have a monumental task before me because God chose a thirty-seven-year-old nobody like me to reveal all these things. I would have never thought that God would pick someone like me. I felt that if I have anything coming from God it would definitely be His judgment for the wrongdoing I engaged in. Well God had mercy on me and gave me a job to give a word to the world, and I am ready to do what God has sent me to do.

Chapter 1

One of the biggest problems in Christianity today is the misinterpretation of the Bible. It saddens me that we have allowed philosophy, dogma, and speculation to enter our minds, causing us to lose sight of the true meaning of God's Word. As Christians, we have been receiving and passing down philosophy, dogma, and speculation for generations. This has also caused far too much confusion, division, and separation between Christians and churches around the world.

I am very grateful, humbled and happy to say that God has given me mind-blowing revelations that opened my understanding of His Word to share with the world.

The impact of these revelations not only opened my understanding, but also caused me to see that God gives revelation and understanding to whomever He chooses. It does not matter if you have read the Bible over twenty times. If God does not open your understanding, or give you revelation, you will end up speculating about the things you do not completely understand.

I have noticed that once people come upon some tough questions that they cannot answer, they have the tendency to speculate to make sense of what they read. I have a problem with this because most speculation sounds very good and it fits the Scripture at hand. This is also a big problem because people build their doctrine on these speculations that have diverted them from the true meaning of God's Word.

In this book, I tear down *speculations* while filling the empty spaces with *revelations*. For example, in Genesis 4:1-5, Cain and Abel both brought offerings to the Lord. The Lord respected Abel's offering, but the Lord did not respect Cain's offering.

WHY IS THAT?

The first thing we are going to do is look at some of the speculations people use, and then we will erase all the speculations and replace them with revelation.

Speculation 1

Some theologians say that Abel brought the very best that he had, but Cain did not bring the very best that he had, but only what he wanted to bring, and that is why the Lord did not respect Cain's offering.

Speculation 2

Some theologians say that Abel had a good heart, but Cain had an improper heart and attitude, and that is why the Lord did not respect Cain's offering.

Speculation 3

Some theologians say that Abel brought blood for his offering because the Lord requires blood for sin sacrifices, but Cain did not bring blood, and that is why the Lord did not respect Cain's offering.

Speculation 4

Some theologians say that the Lord did not respect Cain's offering because Cain's offering was the work of his own hands.

I know there are more speculations about Cain and Abel's offering that I have not mentioned that people believe to be true.

Let us erase all these speculations and replace them with revelation. The first thing I want you to understand is the word respect. The Hebrew word respect means *to pay attention to* and *to look upon with favor*. I also want you to keep in mind that the Bible will interpret itself.

Now, the answer to why Cain's offering was not *respected (looked upon with favor)* is found in Genesis 3:17.

Verse 17:*"Then to Adam He said, because you have heeded the voice of your wife, and have eaten from the tree of which I commanded you saying you shall not eat of it **cursed is the ground for your sake.**"*

So, Cain brought the *fruit of the ground* that the Lord had just cursed, and tried to offer it to the Lord, but the Lord did not respect it because the ground was cursed (spotted and blemished). This is also a picture, but I will not go into the details of pictures at this time. However, all pictures in the Bible are so amazing and perfect, and are there to confirm Scripture.

Now some theologians and scholars may ask, "Why then was the Lord respecting the offering from the ground in Leviticus?" That is a very good question. Let us find out why.

In the genealogy of Adam, Genesis 5:28-29 tells us something that is very important in relation to this topic:

- Verse 28: *"Lamech lived one hundred and eighty-two years, and had a son."*

- Verse 29: *"And he called his name Noah, saying, **"This one will comfort us concerning our work and the toil of our hands because of the ground which the Lord has cursed."***

So now, we see in Genesis 5:28-29 that Noah is going to play a part in fixing the problem dealing with the cursed ground.

I believe that everyone knows what Noah is famous for — *the flood*. We all know that the Lord told Noah to build an ark to save himself and his family from the floodwaters that were coming down on the earth. I believe that we all know what *water* represents in the Bible. However, for those who do not know what *water* represents, it represents *washing* and *cleansing*. After the Lord flooded the earth with *water*, Noah and his family and all the animals exited the ark.

So now, look at what the Lord tells Noah in Genesis 8:20-21:

- Verse 20: *"Then Noah built an altar to the Lord, and took of every clean animal and of every clean bird, and offered burnt offerings on the altar."*

- Verse 21: *"And the Lord smelled a soothing aroma. Then the Lord said in His heart,* **"I will never again curse the ground for man's sake**; *although the imagination of man's heart is evil from his youth."*

Therefore, from that point on, the Lord respected the offering that came from the ground. We no longer have to speculate why Cain's offering was not respected.

As far as Abel bringing an animal with the shedding of its blood for an offering, it is a beautiful and powerful picture of what God will do for us with Jesus later on down the road.

I want you to understand fully that Cain and Abel both brought an *offering*, not a <u>sacrifice for sin</u>.

The Law was not given, or added until Moses' time in Exodus 20.

However, we can see all the beautiful pictures from the beginning of Genesis. This shows the power of God's Word when God said, *"I am God, there is none like me, declaring the end from the beginning, and from ancient times the things that are not yet done,"* in Isaiah 46:9-10.

It is very important that we do not get confused with the pictures in the Bible and assume that Cain and Abel knew about sin offerings, or the Law of Moses. All the beautiful pictures are there from the beginning to give us conformation and for us to see that God had a plan for salvation from the beginning.

I believe we all know that the Law was added because of sin (Galatians 3:19). But, when was the Law added?

The Law was added in Moses' time around two thousand five hundred years after Cain and Abel, and four hundred thirty years after the promises to Abraham (Galatians 3:17), and we cannot, and should not, assume that people knew about the Law before it was given to Moses around 1500BC.

I know the pictures in the Bible can be a little confusing without *"rightly dividing the word of truth."* I am one hundred percent sure that after you finish receiving these revelations that God has given for our time, you will have a better understanding of God's Word, and where you stand as a Christian.

You should understand that the Bible is so powerful and perfect that if we were to wait on God to give us understanding on things we do not know, or fully understand at the time, we would never have to speculate again. It is okay to say you do not know the answer.

Now, I can just imagine the struggles that pastors have when their church members come to them with Biblical questions and they do not have the answers. And, because of their position, they feel obligated to have all the answers to all the questions, and so ninety-five percent of them will speculate. And, when your mind is flooded with speculation, it is almost impossible to receive a revelation because it will mean tearing down a lot of doctrine that was built on those speculations.

That was just an example and a glimpse of some of the most profound and powerful revelations that God has given me to share with you. I have even limited my vocabulary so that everyone can understand what I am sharing. I realize that it is not about boasting with my vocabulary, or what I come to call IMPRESSIVE WORDS, but it is about making sure that the educated as well as the uneducated receive understanding.

It is not about sending an uneducated person to the dictionary every minute trying to get understanding of words that can be reduced or replaced with more simple words for their understanding as well.

Well, in this book, you will not have that problem.

I will make sure that you have a good understanding of all the revelations that were revealed to me.

By the grace of God, this book is packed with mind-blowing revelations, offering a better understanding of God's Word and how to read the Bible in the light from which it is written. After you finish reading the remainder of these revelations, you will never have to ask these or other like questions:

- Who is going to Heaven?
- Who is going to hell?
- Who are the chosen ones?
- Are we the elect?
- Can I lose my salvation?
- Do I have to be water baptized to go to Heaven?
- Is it, "Once saved, always saved?"
- Are we spiritual Israel, or Gentiles?
- Who is going to inherit the earth?

This book will give you the answers you need to know where you stand as a Christian, as well as the *five keys* to understanding the Bible. I will take you through parts of the Bible that people have been misinterpreting for generations, as well as Scriptures that have been taken out of context. I do not believe people misunderstand or take the Scriptures out of context intentionally, but only because of the speculation, they have accepted as truth, they build their doctrine on it, which causes them to see the Scriptures the wrong way. I know now that God is in control of everything, and only gives understanding and revelations for His own reasons, in His own timing and for His own purposes. I do not know why God chose me, of all people—*a nobody*—to reveal all these things, especially when I could think of a lot more powerful and greater men of God that He could have chosen to reveal all these things.

Now, do not get me wrong. I am very thankful and humbled to be able to help people understand the Bible, and bring unity among the people of God.

I encourage all of you to get out your Bibles, and follow along so that you are not taking my word for it, but the Word of God *in context*.

I remember reading some books where the writers took a little part of a Scripture and made it say what they wanted it to say. When the Bible did not fit what their needs, they looked for another Bible translation that came close, or said what they wanted it to say to the point that they had to use five different translations to fit their doctrine, and their points, which is why I encourage you to follow along with your Bible.

Before I start, and give you the topic of the study, I want you to know that God's Word is perfect, there are no contradictions in the Bible at all, and there are thousands of pictures in the Bible to confirm God's Word.

I remember a guy named Rob told me that he believes the Old Testaments is inspired by God, but the New Testaments is not inspired by God. He also said that he does believe that the New Testament has some kind of truth to it.

"Why do you believe that?" I asked him.

He said, "The four gospels contradict each other."

When I asked him to show me where, he took me to the four accounts dealing with the resurrection of Jesus, and what Mary saw at the tomb.

So we both turned to the gospels. And in the gospel of **MATTHEW,** it says that when Mary got to the tomb, an angel rolled back the stone from the front of the tomb and sat on it.

Then we turned to the gospel of **MARK** and it says that Mary saw a young man in a white robe on the inside of the tomb sitting on the right side.

Then we turned to the gospel of **LUKE** and it says that

when Mary got to the tomb there were two men in shining garment standing outside of the tomb.

Then we turned to the gospel of **JOHN** and it says that when Mary got to the tomb there were two angels inside the tomb, one at the feet and one at the head where Jesus was.

Then Rob said, "See! I told you that the Bible in the New Testament has contradictions in it, and its not inspired by God."

At that time, I was a little shaken up because I just knew in my God-given heart that God's Word has no contradictions, and that God's Word is perfect, and true in every way from start to finish. I already knew that God would reveal the answer to me when He was ready, but I wanted the answer right then so that I could explain it to Rob. So I went away with all that on my mind.

I then began to think about how most theologians say that the four gospels are four different perspectives of what each writer saw from their own view, but I was never able to accept that theory because it does not make any sense to me.

It is either Mary saw *one angel roll back the stone and sat upon it,* or she saw *a young man inside the tomb sitting on the right side,* or she saw *two men standing outside the tomb,* or she saw *two angels inside the tomb, one at the feet and one at the head where Jesus was.* And on top of that, the Bible is inspired by God, so why aren't they all saying the same thing?

Well, when God gave me revelation on this, I was just blown away! I am still trying to digest all the revelations that God has given me to share with the world. And because I was never able to contact Rob to explain this particular subject to him, I will explain it to you, and hope that this book reaches him so that he can see that God's Word is perfect, and that there *is no contradiction* in the Bible.

I am going to give you a quick overview of this so that you can see how powerful, perfect, true, and real God's Word is. You will also see that there is no contradiction in the Bible. I am not going to take you too far into the details because there are too many details to explain. However, I will give you enough to understand why the four gospels say exactly what they say, and that God inspires all the New Testament, as well as the Old Testament. And afterwards, we will start the study that will open up your understanding of the Bible.

Okay, let us first look at the four accounts in the Bible about the tomb.

Account 1: Matthew 28:
- Verse 2: *"And, behold, there was a great earthquake; for an angel of the Lord descended from heaven, and rolled back the stone from the door and sat on it."*
- Verse 3: *"His countenance was like lightning and his clothing as white as snow."*

Account 2: Mark 16:
- Verse 5: *"And entering the tomb, they saw a young man clothed in a long white robe sitting on the right side; and they were alarmed."*

Account 3: Luke 24:
- Verse 4: *"And it happened as they were greatly perplexed about this that behold, two men stood by them in shining garments."*

Account 4: John 20:

- Verse 11: *"But Mary stood outside by the tomb weeping, and as she wept she stooped down and looked into the tomb."*

- Verse 12, *"And she saw two angels in white sitting one at the head, and the other at the feet where the body of Jesus had lain."*

Now that we have read the four accounts of what happened when Mary got to the tomb, we are going to look at **four distinct prophesies,** and the Hebrew word **semah**, which is the word for **branch**, which is only found **four times** in the Bible.

Jeremiah 23:5: *"Behold, the days are coming, says the Lord, that I will raise unto David a **branch of righteousness; a king** shall reign and prosper, and execute judgment and righteousness in the earth."*

- Zechariah 3:8: *"Hear now, O Joshua, the high priest, you and your companions who sit before you for they are a wondrous sign; for behold I am bringing forth **my servant the branch.**"*

- Zechariah 6:12: *"Then speak to him saying, "Thus says the Lord of host, saying,* **behold the man whose name is the branch.**"

- Isaiah 4:2: *"In that day* **the branch of the Lord** *be beautiful and glorious."*

We have read the *only four places* the Hebrew word *semah* is found in the Bible. These *four distinct prophecies* are very important, and very powerful. Let us take a closer look at these *four distinct prophecies*:

- Jeremiah 23:5: **BRANCH, a king**
- Zechariah 3:8: **My servant the BRANCH**
- Zechariah 6:12: **The man whose name is the BRANCH**
- Isaiah 4:2: **The BRANCH of the Lord**

A closer look:

1. Branch-king
2. Branch-servant
3. Branch-man
4. Branch-god

The *four gospels* are *four aspects* of Jesus Christ fulfilling these *four distinct prophecies* all at the same time.

- The Gospel of Matthew portrays Jesus as **KING**.
- The Gospel of Mark portrays Jesus as **SERVANT**.
- The Gospel of Luke portrays Jesus as **MAN**.
- The Gospel of John portrays Jesus as **GOD**.

Each writer—Matthew, Mark, Luke and John—characteristically fit a part of the description of who they portray Jesus to be.

MATTHEW—JESUS AS KING

Matthew, who portrays Jesus as *King*, fits a part of the description. Matthew was a *government official*. Matthew starts with a genealogy that links Jesus to David of whom the *King* will come.

In addition, the Gospel of Matthew is the only place you will find *the Kingdom of Heaven* because it deals with Jesus as the earthly *King*. You will not find *the Kingdom of Heaven* in the other gospels; you will only find *the Kingdom of God*.

So, when Mary makes it to the tomb in Matthew 28:2-3, we see that an angel rolled back the *stone* from the door and *sat upon it, his countenance was like lightning.* Now, this is a picture of *Jesus sitting on the throne as king.*

MARK—JESUS AS SERVANT

Mark, who portrays Jesus as a *servant*, fits a part of the description. Mark was a *servant* to Peter, and a *servant* to the apostle Paul. Mark does not record a genealogy.

Now, when Mary makes it to the tomb, inside she sees a *young man* clothed in a long, white robe sitting on the right side. This is a picture of Jesus ready to serve.

LUKE—JESUS AS MAN

Luke, who portrays Jesus as *man,* fits a part of the description. Luke was a *physician,* a person who knows a lot about the human body. Luke has a genealogy that links Jesus back to Adam, showing that Jesus was *man.* Throughout Luke, the phrase: *"the son of man"* is written at least twenty-six times.

Now, when Mary makes it to the tomb, she sees *two*

men standing by in shining garments. This is a picture of Jesus as *man*. Jesus said, in Matthew 18:16, *"by the mouth of **two** or three witness every word may be established.* "So in Luke, there are ***two men*** who talk to Mary at the tomb about the risen Lord.

JOHN—JESUS AS GOD

John, who portrays Jesus as *God*, fits a part of the description. John was the *beloved* or *the one who Jesus loved*. John starts with a *spiritual genealogy* that links Jesus *straight to God himself*:

"In the beginning was the Word, and the Word was with God, and the Word was God." — John 1-1

Well, we know the *Word* became flesh, which was *Jesus Christ*. Throughout the Gospel of John, we see that Jesus uses *I am* from Exodus 3:14 and *I am he* from Isaiah 43:10 and 43:14.

Jesus says in John 8:58, *"Most assuredly, I say to you, before Abraham was, **I am**."*

We also see Jesus using the phrase *I am he* in John 18:4-8 that made all the troops and officers from the chief priest and Pharisees fall to the ground, which also shows the power of *God* speaking. We also know that anyone trying to show that Jesus was *God* in the flesh will take you to the Gospel of John.

Now, when Mary makes it to the tomb, she **looks inside** and sees ***two angels, one at the head and one at the feet where Jesus' body had lain.*** This is a picture of the ***mercy seat*** that Moses was to make in Exodus 25:17-22.

As we know, all the Scriptures pointed to Jesus Christ, and all the ***prophecies*** had to be fulfilled in the ***one*** person, Jesus, all at the same time. We can see now why we have to have ***four different aspects*** of Jesus while He was on earth.

I believe we know that if prophecy says *a king* will come and reign and prosper, and execute judgment and righteousness in the earth (Jeremiah 23:5), then that is exactly what will happen, *a king* will come.

We know that a *king* rules, and executes judgment. A *king* does not *serve*, but rather has servants.

Prophecy also *says "behold, I am bringing forth **my** servant the branch."* That is exactly what will happen. A ***servant*** will come. We all know that a ***servant*** serves, and does not rule, or execute judgment.

So, if Jesus is fulfilling all the prophecies, all at the same time, ***we have to have the four different aspects of***

Jesus while he was on earth. God also put all the beautiful pictures in the Bible to confirm everything.

So we see that God's Word is perfect, there are *no contradictions* at all in God's Word, and the whole Bible is inspired by God.

Okay, now we are going to start our study so that we can have the right understanding of the Bible because something went wrong and we are going to see firsthand what that something is.

Do you know that we have over thirty-seven thousand different denominations in Christianity today? I know you can recall the apostle Paul attacking this same problem in the church of Corinth around 56AD, when the believers were separating themselves from each other. One group says, "I am of Paul." And another says, "I am of Apollos," and another says, "I am of Cephas (Peter)." And another says, "I am of Christ." (1 Corinthians 1:12.)

Now here we are in the twenty-first century and we still have over thirty-seven thousand denominations saying the same thing: Baptist, Protestant, Apostolic, Catholic, Mormon, Jehovah's Witness, Latter Day Saints, Church Of

God In Christ, Assembly Of Yahweh, Secrets Of Yahweh, The Feast Keepers, Sabbatarian, Pentecostal, Sacred Name Movement, Calvinists, and the list goes on.

SOMETHING WENT TERRIBLY WRONG!

Every church is divided by denominations. And what I find to be even more devastating is the fact that every denomination feels one hundred percent that they have the truth, and that they are the true church of today. Do you know what this does to people? This forces a baby Christian, or new believer, to try to decipher what church is the *right* or *true* church.

I can remember crying out to God, and asking Him why we have so many denominations in Christianity? Well, I can tell you this, God showed me the reason, and where people go wrong. So now, I will share with you everything that God has revealed to me.

Chapter 2

The first thing I am going to do is give you the topic of this study. The topic is also a question and one that every pastor, preacher, teacher, Christian, and theologian has to ask themselves to fully understand the Bible.

The topic is,

WHY THE APOSTLE PAUL?

We have to ask ourselves this question. I do not care who you are, or how much you think you know about the Bible. If you are studying the Bible for understanding to minister, preach, and teach, you have to ask this question: Why the apostle Paul?

The reason why we have to ask this question is that we know that Jesus came and handpicked *twelve apostles* because there were *twelve tribes of Israel*. And these twelve apostles will be sitting on twelve thrones judging the twelve tribes of Israel, Matthew 19:28 and Luke 22:28-30.

I believe everyone knows that if one of the twelve apostles was taken out, that another person would have to take his place (Acts 1:22).We also know that Judas was numbered with the twelve apostles and that he was the one who betrayed Jesus, which led to his death.

And because of that, it left them with only eleven apostles, which confirms Psalms 109:8 that says, *"Let his days be few and **let another take his office**."*

So now, we see in Acts 1:15-26 the need for them to pick another person to complete the twelve apostles. I also want you to note that there were two men to choose from—Joseph called Barsabas, who was surnamed Justus, and Matthias—Acts 1:23.

It is very important that we see that even though the two of them qualified to be an apostle, they both could not be an apostle because that would be more than twelve apostles. That would be thirteen apostles when there are only twelve tribes of Israel. So they cast lots to pick one of them, and the lot fell on Matthias, and so Matthias completed the twelve apostles. Acts 1:26 says, *"And so he was numbered with the eleven apostles."* So now, we have the twelve apostles who will be sitting on twelve thrones judging the twelve tribes of Israel. These twelve apostles also have their names written on the wall of the twelve foundations of the city in the New Jerusalem. (Revelation 21:14 says, *"Now the wall of the city had twelve foundations and on them were the names of the* twelve apostles *of the Lamb.*

Okay, so now we have what appears to be a big problem because Paul was an apostle, according to Romans 1:1, 1 Corinthians 1:1, 2 Corinthians 1:1, Galatians 1:1, Ephesians 1:1, Romans 11:3, Colossians 1:1, 1 Timothy 1:1, 2 Timothy 1:1 and Titus 1:1. Which means Paul will make the thirteenth apostle because Paul was not one of the twelve apostles.

And 1 Corinthians 15:5 and 15:7-8 confirms this to be one hundred percent true.

So, why is it that the apostle Paul does not have his name written on the wall in Revelation 21:14?

Why the apostle Paul will not be sitting on a throne judging one of the twelve tribes of Israel? I have asked the question once, and I will ask it again. Why the apostle Paul?

What is so different and distinct about the apostle Paul from the twelve apostles? How and where does the apostle Paul fit into the Scriptures? Understanding these questions is one of the *five keys* to understanding the Bible.

What I want to do at this time is make sure that we all know what "The Gospel" is. It is very important that we all know what our gospel is. The apostle Paul tells us what the gospel is throughout all of his letters. We can see the gospel very clear in 1 Corinthians 15:1-4:

- Verse 1: *"Moreover, brethren, I declare to you **the gospel** which I preached unto you, which also you have received and in **which you stand**."*

- Verse 2: *"**By which also you are saved,** if you hold fast that word which I preached to you—unless you believed in vain."*

- Verse 3: *"For I delivered to you first of all that which I also received;* **that Christ died for our sins** *according to the scriptures."*

- Verse 4: *"And that* **he was buried** *and that* **he rose again the third day** *according to the scriptures."*

Well, that is the gospel in a nutshell—the **death, burial,** and **resurrection.** We **died** with Christ, were **buried** with Christ, and we **rose** with Christ.

The apostle Paul says in 1 Corinthians 1:2, *"For I determined not to know anything among you except Christ and Him* **crucified.***"*

We also see that the apostle Paul tells the church in Galatians 1:8-9, that *"if anyone preaches* **any other gospel** *to you than what we have preached to you let him be accursed."*

So now that we know what the gospel is, I have a question for you. Were the twelve apostles preaching this gospel? Well, we are going to find out together. Let us turn to Luke 9:1-6). This is the first recording in Luke where Jesus sends out the twelve apostles to preach the gospel to the people.

- Verse 1: *"Then He called His twelve disciples together and gave them power and authority over all demons, and to cure diseases."*
- Verse 2 : *"He sent them to preach the kingdom of God and heal the sick."*
- Verse 3 : *"And He said to them, "take nothing for the journey, neither staff nor bag nor bread nor money: and do not have two tunics apiece."*
- Verse 4 : *"Whatever house you enter, stay there, and from there depart."*
- Verse 5 : *"And whoever will not receive you, when you go out of that city, shake off the very dust from your feet as a testimony against them."*
- Verse 6 : *"So they departed and went through the towns, preaching **the gospel** and healing everywhere."*

Okay, so we see that the twelve apostles were preaching the gospel. Now let us turn to Luke 18:31-34. This is the third time Jesus predicts His death.

- Verse 31: *"Then He took the **twelve** aside and said to them, "Behold, we are going up to Jerusalem, and all things that are written by the prophets concerning the Son of Man will be accomplished."*
- Verse 32: *"For He will be delivered to the Gentiles and will be mocked and insulted and spit upon."*
- Verse 33: *"They will scourge Him and **kill Him** and the **third day He will rise again.**"*
- That is the gospel right there—the *death, burial* and the resurrection, but take a look at what happens in the very next verse.
- Verse 34: ***"But they understood none of these things; this saying was hidden from them, and they did not know the things that were spoken."***

So now, we have a problem. The twelve apostles were going around preaching the gospel for three years while Jesus was on the earth, but they never knew that Jesus was going to *die,* and be *buried,* and *rise* again on the third day, which of course is the gospel by which *we stand* and by which *we are saved.*

So, if the *twelve apostles* never knew about Jesus' *death, burial and resurrection,* which is *the gospel* that *we stand by* and *that saves us,* then what *gospel* were the *twelve apostles* going around preaching for three years?

What *gospel* were the seventy that Jesus sent out, two by two, preaching, and who was that *gospel* to?

We just found out that the *twelve apostles* and the seventy that Jesus sent out were not preaching *the gospel* that *we stand by and that saves us,* but they still went through the towns preaching *the gospel* to the people.

Now this is very clear because not only was Jesus still alive, and hadn't died yet, while the twelve apostles and the seventy were preaching the gospel, but Jesus also told His twelve apostles a couple of times that He was going to *die,* and *rise* again, but it was hidden from them. And they still did not know that Jesus was going to *die* and *rise* again. This is another one of the *five keys* to understanding the Bible.

Before we go any deeper into the study of the apostle Paul—the twelve *apostles,* and the *gospel* they were preaching, I want to make sure you understand what Old

Testament and New Testament mean, as well as when the Old Testament ends and the New Testament begins. This is extremely important because people who do not understand when the Old Testament ends and the New Testament begins have thought that the Old Testament was for the Jews, and the New Testament was for us (the Gentiles). And that we are "spiritual Israel." This is a big misinterpretation of Scripture that we will see as we go along.

The first thing I want to make sure that you know, and fully understand, is the word *testament*. The Greek word for *testament* is diathéké, and it only means *covenant*. In other words, when you hear or see Old Testament, or New Testament, it is only saying Old Covenant and New Covenant.

For those who do not know, the Old Covenant is the covenant God made with the children of Israel at Mount Sinai when they came out of the land of Egypt (Exodus 20-24).

As we all know, the children of Israel did not keep the covenant, and they were rebellious continually, and God scattered them into all the nations just as God said He would do in Leviticus 26:33. God also said that He will go after the children of Israel and gather them from all the nations, and bring them back to *their own land* (Ezekiel 37:21 and 26:24; Jeremiah 31:10). On top of that, God promised the children of Israel a New Covenant (Jeremiah 31:31).

Now, I want you to pay close attention to who this *New Covenant is promised.*

Jeremiah 31:31: *"Behold, the days are coming, says the LORD, when I will make a* **New Covenant with the house of Israel, and the house of Judah."**

- Verse 32: *"Not according to the* **covenant** *that I made with their fathers in the day that* **I** *took them by the hand to lead them out of the land of Egypt, My* **covenant** *which they broke, although I was a husband to them, says the Lord."*

- Verse 33: *"But this is the* **covenant** *that I will make with the* **house of Israel** *after those days, says the Lord: I will put my law in their minds, and write it on their hearts; and I will be their God, and they shall be my people."*

- Verse 34: *"No more shall every man teach his neighbor, and say" know the Lord, for they all shall know Me, from the least of them to the greatest of them, says the Lord. For I will forgive their iniquity, and their sin; I will remember no more."*

So now, we see who the New Covenant was made to: the house of Israel and the house of Judah.

This is very important to understand, and as we continue, you will see why. So here we have the New Covenant, which is the indwelling of the Holy Spirit promised to the house of Israel and the house of Judah.

My next question to you is, When did the promised New Covenant or New Testament start? Most people think that the New Testament or New Covenant started in Matthew 1:1, Mark 1:1, Luke 1:1 and John 1:1. This is a big misunderstanding.

The New Testament or New Covenant did not start until Jesus died on the cross, and said, *"It is finished,"* John 19:30. Neither could it start while Jesus was still on the earth because *Jesus' blood* is the *blood* of the New Covenant or New Testament, which is the indwelling of the Holy

Spirit.

So now, we can fully understand what Jesus is saying in John 16:7, *"Nevertheless I tell you the truth.* ***It is to your advantage that I go away; for if I do not go away, the helper****(Holy Spirit)* ***will not come to you;*** *but if I depart, I will send Him to you."*

So now, we can see and understand that the New Covenant or New Testament could not start until Jesus shed His blood.

It is very important to understand that the whole time Jesus was on the earth, He was under the Old Covenant, which is the *Law of Moses*(Galatians 4:4-5). Jesus had to fulfill the Old Covenant by obeying it perfectly. Jesus also taught the people to obey it as well. St Matthew 5:17-19 says:

- Verse 17: *"Do not think that I came to destroy the* ***law*** *or the prophets. I did not come to destroy but to fulfill."*

- Verse 18: *"For assuredly, I say to you, till heaven and earth pass away, one jot or one tittle will by no means pass from the* ***law*** *till all is fulfilled."*

- Verse 19: *"Whoever therefore breaks one of the least of these commandments, and teaches men so, shall be called least in the kingdom of heaven; but **whoever does and teaches them**, he shall be called great in the kingdom of heaven."*

Jesus, the twelve apostles and all the people they were preaching the gospel to were still under the law or Old Covenant.

So my question is, What gospel were they preaching, and to whom were they preaching? The reason why I have to ask this question is because I was never under the law, or the Old Covenant, nor was I ever promised a New Covenant because I am a Gentile, who is saved by grace through faith, and not a Jew to whom all of the promises were made to.

Now of course this leads me to my next important question. Could Jesus and the twelve apostles have been preaching a gospel that was not for the Gentiles?

Well, according to most theologians, Jesus came to *"everybody"* when he was on the earth—Jews and Gentiles. They also believed that there were Gentiles, as well as Jews present every time Jesus taught the multitudes of people. We are going to take a closer look and see what is going on, and who this gospel is to.

In Matthew, starting at Chapter 5, Verse 1, Jesus goes up on a mountain and starts His first teaching to the multitudes of people. The teaching goes on into Chapter 6 and ends in Chapter 7, Verse 27. However, in Chapter 6, Verses 31 and 32, Jesus says something very interesting.

- Verse 31: *"Therefore do not worry saying, "what shall we eat?' Or" what shall we drink?" Or "what shall we wear?"*

- Verse 32: *"For after all these things **the Gentiles** seek. For your heavenly Father knows that you need all these things."*

Now hold on just one minute because I am a Gentile, and it does not look like Jesus is talking to me, or the Gentiles, rather Jesus is talking about the Gentiles to the people He's teaching. This does not make any sense, especially if Jesus came to the Gentiles while He was on earth. Well, let us look a little closer so that we can see what is going on. Turn three pages over to Matthew 10:1.

This is the first time Jesus sends out the twelve apostles to preach the gospel to the people.

- Verse 1:*"And when He had called His twelve disciples to Him, He gave them power over unclean spirits, to cast them out, and to heal all kinds of sickness and all kinds of disease."*

Now this should have brought joy and happiness to everybody at that time because the twelve apostles are getting ready to go out to the people, preach the gospel, heal people, and cure them of all kinds of diseases. Everything sounds real good until we get to Verses 5 and 6.

- Verse 5:*"These twelve Jesus sent out and commanded them saying,* **Do not go into the way of the Gentiles,** *and do not enter a city of the Samaritans."*

- Verse 6: **"But go rather to the lost sheep of the house of Israel."**

Now hold on just one minute. You mean to tell me that Jesus gave the twelve apostles power to heal *any kind of sickness* and *any kind of disease,* but they were *not to go to the Gentiles,* but to only go to the *house of Israel*(the Jews)?Well, guess what? That is exactly what is going on here. I know that it may seem a little shocking, but it is true.

When Jesus was on the earth, He came to *His own* the Jews (John 1:11). The whole time Jesus was on the earth, He was teaching *His own people* (the Jews) who were under the *law* at the time, as well as fulfilling prophecy at the same time. Jesus did not come to the *Gentiles* while He was on the earth, but the Jews only. In fact, let us turn six pages over to Chapter 15 and see what happened when a Gentile came to Jesus for help (Matthew 15:21-28).

- Verse 21:*"Then Jesus went out from there and departed to the region of Tyre and Sidon."*

- Verse 22 : *"And behold, a woman of Canaan (GENTILE WOMAN) came from that region and cried out to Him, saying,"* **have mercy on me O Lord, son of David!** *My daughter is severely demon possessed."*

Now we all know that if anything is going to move Jesus, it will be *faith, mercy,* and asking for *help*. Well, let us read on and see what Jesus is going to do for the Gentile woman.

- Verse 23: *"But He answered her not a word. And His disciples came and urged Him saying **"send her away, for she cries out after us."***

Now hold the phone for one minute. You mean to tell me that this Gentile woman came begging for *mercy* from Jesus, and Jesus just ignored her as if she was not even there?

And on top of that, Jesus' loving twelve apostles that just came back from preaching the gospel, healing people from all kinds of diseases, and casting out demons tells Jesus to send her away? In other words, *get rid of her.*

I just know now we all are expecting Jesus to rebuke the twelve apostles for saying *"send her away"* instead of helping the Gentile woman, especially when Jesus came for *"everybody"* as some theologians say.

So what is Jesus' response?

- Verse 14: *"But He answered and said, "**I was not sent except to the lost sheep of the house of Israel.**"*

So here, we see Jesus straight out telling the Gentile woman that He was only sent to the lost sheep of the house of Israel(the Jews). Then, of course, the woman gets even more desperate for help in Verse 25.

- Verse 25:*"Then she came and **worshiped** Him, saying "Lord help me!"*

The Greek word for *worshiped* in this verse is *proskyneo*, and it means *to show reverence; to kneel down*.

So now, we have this Gentile woman begging on her knees for help. I just know that this had to move Jesus to help her because the woman strongly believed and knew, for a fact, that Jesus could help her.

And on top of that, the Gentile woman was showing a lot of *faith*. Well, let us keep reading and see what Jesus said.

- Verse 26: *"But He answered and said,* **"It is not good to take the children's bread and throw it to the little dogs."**

Now hold the phone, and the bus. You mean to tell me that Jesus just called this begging, helpless, on her knees, faith having Gentile woman a *dog*? Now I know that it was common for Jews, back in their time, to call the

Gentiles dogs, or animals, or unclean people, but this is Jesus talking here. What is going on? What is Jesus doing?

Well, for those who do not know, the *bread* is Jesus Himself, and the *children* are the Israelites (Jews) and the *dogs* are the *Gentiles*. Now, it would seem to me that the Gentile Woman would have gotten offended by Jesus' words and gotten up and walked away. Well, she did not, so let us look at her response.

- Verse 27:*"And she said "yes, Lord, yet even the little dogs eat the crumbs which fall from their masters table."*

Well, here we see that the woman recognizes that she is a Gentile and not a Jew to whom all of the promises were made. She recognized that salvation is of the Jews, just like Jesus told the woman at the well. In other words, she is saying, "Can I get a little crumb or peace of *Israel's* blessings?"

And, of course, Jesus says yes by Verse 28. This is also a picture of what was coming to the Gentiles once Israel had gotten cast away.

It's very important to understand that Jesus already

knew that Israel was going to reject Him as their king, and that the salvation of God was going to go to the Gentiles, but at the time, salvation was of the Jews, and Jesus is only sent to the Jews. Salvation had not yet been sent to the Gentiles.

Even though Jesus may have healed a couple of Gentiles, they still did not have *salvation,* and *"the gospel"* that was being preached at that time was to the Jews only.

Yes! I know that for God so loved *the world* that He gave His only begotten Son that *whoever believes in Him will have everlasting life.* Yes! I know that Jesus came to save *everybody,* but everybody missed the *process.* And because of this, *three major things happened that threw everybody off on their doctrine, and understanding of the Bible.*

The first thing that threw everybody off was the combining of the *two gospels.* We have combined *Israel's kingdom gospel* with our *grace gospel,* and it threw everybody off. The second major thing that we have done is combined *the kingdom of heaven* with the *heavenlies,* and it threw everybody off as well. The third major thing that threw everybody off is we have combined *prophecy* with *mystery.* Now we can all see why the apostle Paul said to *"rightly divide the word of truth"* (2 Timothy 2:15).

Thirty-seven thousand denominations came out of combining these three major things together. One of the biggest confusions that came out of combining the *two gospels* was *baptism*. We have all different ways and different reasons to *water baptize* a person. One church says that you have to baptize a person while they are a baby. Another church says that you have to sprinkle them with water to baptize them. Other churches say that you have to pour the water on their heads three times to baptize them. Then we have the churches that say you have to submerge them under water because the Greek word baptizo means *to dip*. Then, of course, we have the churches that agree on the submerging, but they argue amongst themselves on which *name* is the right name to baptize in. One church says that you have to baptize in the *name of the Father, the Son, and the Holy Ghost* because Jesus said it Himself in Matthew 28:19. Then the other church says, *No!* That is a title, and we have to baptize in the *name of Jesus* because Peter said it in Acts 2:38, and because of what Jesus said in

John 3:5; it has to be done to enter the kingdom of heaven. Then, we have the churches that say, *"Baptism is an outward expression of an inward conversion."*

Now we all know that the Bible does not say, or teach that, and that is because it is not true at all. However, it does sound good and it even seems as if it fits, but this is *speculation*, and as we go along we will erase and replace all this *confusion* and *speculation* with *revelation*.

Chapter 3

In this chapter, we will receive a better understanding about *Israel's kingdom gospel* as we learn what their gospel was, when their gospel started, and when their gospel ended. **Israel's kingdom gospel** started with John the Baptist, and ended the moment they were cast away. And because of their being cast away, the Gentiles were grafted in but without all of the physical ceremonial requirements that Israel had to do.

As we go through the process, you will see why *the apostle Paul* was *raised up* and *set apart* for a specific purpose, and became the dominant apostle to the point that he was able to rebuke Peter who was given the keys of the kingdom of heaven by Jesus Himself. We will also go through some of the parables that we have done a poor job of spiritualizing to fit what we thought they meant, which took away from the powerful impact that they were intended to have when understood in their proper context. And because baptism is tied into Israel's kingdom gospel, I will touch on baptism as well.

To understand Israel's kingdom gospel, we would have to go back to the beginning to see what was promised to them because the Greek word for gospel is evongelion and it means *good news* or *glad tidings*. So for us to fully understand what John the Baptist was doing and preaching, and also all the things that Jesus said, including all the parables that we spiritualize to make sense to us, we would have to go back to the beginning.

I know that most pastors believe that all they have to do is to read from Matthew up to Revelation if they want to preach or teach because the New Testament deals with us Gentiles. Most pastors believe that the Old Testament is not that important, and that we should stay more focused on the New Testament. This is a big misunderstanding because for us to understand the New Testament, we would have to have a good understanding of the Old Testament. People who do not understand the Old Testament will spiritualize everything in the New Testament, including all the parables. I've notice that people who do not have a good understanding of the Old Testament have a lot of trouble understanding most of the things that Jesus said, as well as the parables that Jesus used to the point that they start saying, "Jesus wasn't really saying that," or "Jesus really meant to say this," or "Peter was trying to say this," or "John really didn't mean to say this when he said that." In other words, we try to tell Jesus, Peter, and John the Baptist what they were trying to say, when all the while they said exactly what they meant to say. It is us who lack the *understanding* and the *process* to the point that we come up with all kinds of misleading ideas and doctrines that sound good, and seem to fit, as we stay away from the things that we cannot explain or interpret. As we go through the process of Israel's kingdom gospel, we will receive a better understanding of the things that we could not understand before, as well as the parables that we have also misunderstood. I know I will say some things that will conflict with some of the things that you have accepted as truth, as well as scriptures that you have always looked at in a certain way. However, if you will allow me to put them in the proper order that God has revealed to me, I am sure you will thank God for the revelations as well. I also know that as you read this book, there will be scriptures that pop up in your mind that you may be wondering if I missed, or had not considered them. I can assure you that I have considered everything that might, and will pop up in your mind because they popped up in my mind when God was revealing these things to me as well. I can remember saying to myself, "But what about this scripture," and "What about that scripture," and "What about when Paul said this, or when Jesus said that?" I can tell you that by the time God was through with me, everything became clear. And yes! It took a lot of tearing down speculation, and misinterpretation that I built my doctrine on to see the truth of the scriptures in the right context. So be prepared to do the same.

Before I take you on the journey through Israel's kingdom gospel, I want to point out one of the biggest problems we have when reading the Bible so that you will not get confused as we go through their gospel.

In Chapter 2, I gave you three major things that we have combined that threw everybody off, and one of them was the combining of *prophecy* with *mystery*. It is very important that we do not combine the mystery that the apostle Paul was raised up for, and set apart to proclaim to the world, with Israel's kingdom gospel, which was prophesied throughout the Old Testament.

It is extremely important that you keep in mind, as we go through the process of Israel's kingdom gospel, that the apostle Paul has not yet been raised up to receive the mystery, Israel has not yet been cast away, the Law is still binding at the time of their gospel, and people were being saved without knowing that Jesus was going to die on the cross. I also want you to keep in mind that while Jesus, the twelve apostles, and the seventy that Jesus sent out to preach the gospel to the people were not preaching that Jesus *died for their sins* because Jesus hadn't died yet. Nor were they preaching that Jesus was *going to die for their sins* because nobody knew that either. So let us see what their gospel(good news, or glad tidings) was.

In Genesis 12:1-3, God made a promise to Abram (Abraham).

- Verse 1: *"Now the Lord had said to Abram: Get out of your country, from your family and from your father's house, to a land that I will show you."*

- Verse 2: *"I will make you a great nation; I will bless you and make your name great; and you shall be a blessing."*

- Verse 3: "I will bless those who bless you, and I will curse him who curses you; **and in you all the families of the earth shall be blessed.**"

Keep in mind what the Lord said in Verse 3 about all the families of the earth being blessed through Abram because this is very important, and we will see why as we go through the process.

In Genesis 15:1-6, God makes a covenant with Abram that He would make his descendants as the stars of heaven unable to be counted. By Verse 18, God said that He will give the land that He had given to Abram to his descendants. I also want you to keep in mind that this is physical land on physical earth, and it is not to be spiritualized. By Chapter 17, God changes Abram's name to *Abraham* and tells him that he will be a father of many nations, and gave him the sign of the covenant, which is circumcision. And by Verse 7, God confirms that He will establish His covenant with Abraham's descendants. By Verse 13, God explains to Abraham that his descendants will be in slavery for four hundred years before they receive the inheritance of the promise land that God is giving to them.

Well, of course, the covenant people (Israel)went into bondage for four hundred years, and Moses was raised up to deliver them out of bondage. After God brought them out of the land of Egypt, Moses led them through the wilderness to a mountain called Sinai. Then God told Moses to tell the children of Israel something very interesting in Exodus 19:1-6.

- Verse 1: *"In the third month after the children of Israel had gone out of the land of Egypt, on the same day, they came to the Wilderness of Sinai."*

- Verse 2: *"For they had departed from Rephidim, had come to the Wilderness of Sinai, and camped in the wilderness. So Israel camped there before the mountain."*

- Verse 3: *"And Moses went up to God, and the Lord called to him from the mountain saying, "Thus you shall say to the house of Jacob, and tell the children of Israel;"*

- Verse 4: *"You have seen what I did to the Egyptians, and how I bore you on eagles' wings and brought you to Myself.*

- Verse 5: *"Now therefore, if you will indeed obey My voice and keep My covenant,* **then you shall be a special treasure to Me above all people; for all the earth is Mine.**

- Verse 6: **"And you shall be to Me a kingdom of priests and a holy nation. These are the words which you shall speak to the children of Israel."**

Okay, so let us make sure that we got this right. Israel will be a *special people above all people.* And they will be *a kingdom of priests.* Now we have to confirm this thing about Israel being a *special people above all people* because the apostle Paul said that God does not show *partiality* in Romans 2:11, Galatians 2:6, Ephesians 6:9. So we have to confirm this thing about Israel being a *special people above all people.*

Let us see if we can get some clarity on the issues. Turn with me to the book of Deuteronomy, Chapter 7 where Moses is teaching them on what to do, and how to act when they go in to possess the land that God is giving them. Moses says something very interesting in Verse 6: *"For you are a holy people to the Lord your God;* **the Lord your God has chosen you to be a people for Himself, a special treasure above all the peoples on the face of the earth.***"*

Well, there is no way around that at all. Israel is a special people above all the people on the face of the earth. God said it, Moses confirmed it, and that is exactly what it is. So what is the apostle Paul saying when he says, *"There is no **partiality** with God, or no difference between **Jew** and **Gentile**?"* Well, let me tell you what is going on here. The apostle Paul was raised up and set apart to preach the *mystery* period of grace *after* Israel was casted away. The Greek word for *mystery* is *musterion* and it means *secret, something that is hidden and requires special revelation; something no one ever knew.* Paul preached something that was never prophesied in the Bible. But since we have not gotten to Paul yet, and Israel has not been cast away at the time, we cannot mix the apostle Paul mystery period of grace, with the process of prophecy. And so at that time *Israel was a special people above all the people on the face of the earth.*

Moving right along, in Exodus, Chapters 20 to 23, God makes a covenant with the children of Israel, which is the Law. They were given things to do, as well as things that they could not do. Their covenant came with blessings and curses for obedience and disobedience.

In Chapter 24, the children of Israel confirm the covenant, saying, *"All that the Lord said to do we will do."*

Well, as we all know, the children of Israel did not keep the covenant, and they were disobedient all the time. And even though the children of Israel repeatedly broke the covenant, and God punished them repeatedly, God still loved them and would keep His promises to Abraham, Isaac, and Jacob. God would also keep His promises to the children of Israel because God could not lie.

So even though God scattered the children of Israel throughout all the nations, God repeatedly said that He would go out and gather them from all the nations, and bring them back to their own land. And once again, this is physical land right here on physical earth in physical Jerusalem(Jeremiah 23:3, Jeremiah 29:14, Jeremiah 31:8, Jeremiah 31:10, Jeremiah 32:37, Ezekiel 20:41, Ezekiel 22:19, Ezekiel 34:13, and Ezekiel 36:24).

God also promised them a new covenant (Jeremiah 31:31) and a physical king that will sit on the throne of David right here on physical earth, in physical Jerusalem (Jeremiah 23:5-6).This king will be the Messiah that will save them from their enemies, restore Jerusalem, and bring back the children of Israel from all the nations to their own land, which is Jerusalem, save them from their sins so they don't have to sacrifice animals anymore, and rule on the throne of David as the prophecies proclaimed.

I know that a lot of preachers believe that Jesus is sitting on the throne of David right now in a spiritual sense, and that we (Gentiles) are spiritual Israel, but that is not so. This misunderstanding comes from misinterpreting the apostle Paul's letters, and the lack of understanding the Old Testament. We are not spiritual Israel, and Jesus *is not* sitting on the throne of David, *yet*. Jesus is sitting at the right hand of the Father until his enemies are made His footstool (Hebrews 10:12-13). And we are Gentiles who were grafted in because of Israel's unbelief. I really hope you all understand what was just said. I am going to say it again to make sure that you really understand what this means. *We are gentiles who were grafted in because of Israel's unbelief.* I repeated this a second time because this was never prophesied in the Bible. Prophecy never said that the Gentiles will be saved or grafted in because of Israel's unbelief.

Prophecy says the complete opposite. It was by Israel's acceptance that the Gentiles would come to the light, and Israel would act as a kingdom of Priests to bring all the other nations (Gentiles) to God (Isaiah 60:12 and Zechariah

8:1-23). But something strange happened, prophecy stopped, Israel got cast away, and a mystery period had started, and Paul was raised up to proclaim it. Right now, there is a pause on prophecy, and we are going to look at that pause on prophecy later on in full detail. This is something that is going to blow your mind just as it blew mine. And this is extremely important to understand.

I do not want to jump ahead into the mystery period, but I have to because of the aforementioned, and it is very important that I point this out before we go on through the process of prophecy. Look at what the apostle Paul says in Romans 11:18-20.

- Verse 18 : *"Do not boast against the branches. But if you do boast remember that you do not support the root, but the root supports you."*

- Verse 19:*"You will say then,* **"Branches were broken off that I might be grafted in."**

- Verse 20:*"**Well said. Because of unbelief they were broken off** and you stand by faith. Do not be haughty, but **fear.**"*

The Greek word for *fear* in this verse is *phobeo*, and it means *to be alarmed, scared, frightened, dismayed, and filled with dread*. Now keep in mind that this is the apostle Paul telling us (Gentiles) how we should feel at this time of being saved, and that it happened because of Israel's unbelief.

So, if we are Gentiles that have been grafted in because of Israel's unbelief, then what would have happened if Israel would have believed? Would the Gentiles still have been saved?

Well, so that no one gets scared, let me tell you the answer. YES, the Gentiles would have still been saved, but it would have been the way prophecy said it would happen. And do not get confused on this because prophecy still has to be fulfilled, and it will happen the way prophecy said it will happen. Yes! Ten men will grasp the sleeve of a Jewish man to be led to God (Zechariah 8:23). But, of course, this will happen after the *mystery body of Christ*(the church) is caught up, and prophecy continues. I do not want to go into all the details at this time, because it could be very confusing, without going through the process first. But I will cover all this later on as we come to it. So let us get back to the process of prophecy.

So now, we have the children of *Israel(the special people above all other people on the face of the earth)*who will be a holy nation who is promised: (1) physical land on earth, (2) a physical king that will sit on the throne of David on earth, and (3) a physical heavenly ruled kingdom on earth so that they can be a kingdom of priests to bring the rest of the world (i.e., nations/Gentiles) to God. It is very important that you keep this in mind: *land, king,* and *kingdom.* Now we have to find out what is the process of being a priest because Israel will be a kingdom of priests to the world in the future. We can see the process of what it takes to be a priest by looking at what it took for Aaron and his sons to be priests over Israel.

Let us turn to Leviticus, Chapter 8, which shows the process of what it takes to be a priest. I do recommend that you read the entire chapter because I am going to point out the three steps it took them to be a priest. And I want you to keep this in mind as we proceed to the New Testament.

In Leviticus 8:1-23,

- Verse 1: *"And the Lord spoke to Moses, saying:*

- Verse 2: *"Take Aaron and his sons with him and the garments, the anointing oil, a bull as the sin offering, two rams, and a basket of unleavened bread;*

- Verse 3: *"And gather all the congregation together at the door of the tabernacle of meeting."*

- Verse 4: *"So Moses did as the LORD commanded him. And the congregation was gathered together at the door of the tabernacle of meeting."*

- Verse 5: *"And Moses said to the congregation, "this is what the LORD commanded to be done."*

- Verse 6: *"Then Moses brought Aaron and his sons and **washed them with water**."*

That is the first step. Now drop down to Verse 12 so we can see the next step.

- Verse 12: *"And he **poured some of the anointing oil on Aaron's head** and anointed him, to consecrate him."*

That is the second step. Now drop down to Verse 22.

- Verse 22: *"And he brought the second ram, the ram of consecration. Then Aaron and his sons laid their hands on the head of the ram,*
- Verse 23: *"And Moses killed it.* ***Also he took some of its blood and put it on the tip of Aaron's right ear, on the thumb of his right hand, and on the big toe of his right foot.****"*

That is the last step it took them to be a priest, and so in Chapter 9 they started their role as a priest.

It is very important that you keep these three steps in mind.

1. Wash with water.
2. The pouring of anointing oil on the head.
3. Blood on the ear, hand, and foot.

I know that putting blood on someone's ear, hand, and foot does not make any sense right now, but remember everything that happened in the Old Testament is a picture of something that is coming.

So now, we come to the last prophecy that was prophesied by Malachi. I recommend that you read the book of Malachi who is the last person to prophesy before angelic visitation stopped for four hundred fifty years, as I will only be touching on prophecy that is relevant to the process. Let us look at Malachi 3:1.

- Verse 1:*"Behold, I send My messenger, **and he will prepare the way before me**. And the Lord, whom you seek, will suddenly come to His temple, **even the messenger of the covenant, in whom you delight**. Behold, He is coming says the Lord of hosts."*

Now we see that the messenger is going to come and prepare the way before the Lord. Let us also look at who that messenger will be, according to prophecy. Turn to Malachi 4:5-6.

- Verse 5:*"Behold, I send you **Elijah the prophet** before the coming of the great and dreadful day of the Lord.*

- Verse 6:***"And he will turn the hearts of the fathers to the children,** and the **hearts of the children to their fathers**, lest I come and strike the earth with a curse."*

As we move into what people call the New Testament, we will see how things unfold. Keep in mind everything discussed thus far. Also remember that Matthew, Mark, Luke and John are accounts of the birth of Jesus, and what He did while He was on earth, and they end with His death, burial and resurrection. The New Testament (New Covenant)starts after Jesus died, and resurrected.

As we are reading the gospels, remember that we are still reading the Old Testament, and witnessing the fulfillment of prophecy as it happens.

I want to start in the Book of Luke because Luke portrays Jesus as man, and deals with the birth of the forerunner and the birth of Jesus in detail. Now keep in mind what we just read from the last prophet Malachi, that the one who will come and turn the hearts of the fathers to the children will be Elijah the Prophet. This is very important to keep in mind as we go through the process because we all know that Elijah did not come, but John the Baptist played the part of Elijah.

Let us start at Luke 1:1-4.

- Verse 1: *"Inasmuch as many have taken in hand to **set in order a narrative of those things which have been fulfilled among us,***
- Verse 2: *"Just as those who from the beginning were eyewitnesses and ministers of the word delivered them to us,*
- Verse 3: *"It seemed good to me also, having had perfect understanding of all things from the very first, **to write to you an orderly account**, most excellent Theophilus,*
- Verse 4: *"That you may know the certainty of those things in which you were instructed."*

So here, we see that Luke is writing a narrative to Theophilus to show him everything that happened with Jesus, and all the prophecy that He fulfilled. The first person that Luke starts with is Zacharias, the father of John the Baptist.

For four hundred and fifty years there were no angelic visitations, and then out of the blue, the angel Gabriel appears to Zacharias while he was serving as priest, and tells him that he will have a son, and to name him John. The angel Gabriel also tells him that *"John will be filled with the holy spirit from his mother's womb,"* Verse 15.

This is very important to understand and as we go along, you will see why. Let us read Verses 16 and 17.

- Verse 16:*"And he will turn many of the **children of Israel** to the Lord their God.*

- Verse 17: *"He will also go before Him **in the spirit and power of Elijah,** to **turn the hearts of the fathers to the children,** and the disobedient to the wisdom of the just, **to make ready a people prepared for the Lord."***

We know that the same angel, Gabriel, appeared to the Virgin Mary and told her that she will bear a son as well, and to name Him Jesus (Verse 31).In Verse 32, Gabriel tells Mary that God will give Jesus the throne of His father David. In Chapter 2, Mary gives birth to the child, wraps Him in swaddling clothes and lays Him in a manger. In Verse 8, there are shepherds that hear from an angel of the Lord that the savior who is Christ the Lord has been born.

It is very important that you keep in mind the word *savior* because we are going to see what the children of Israel were being saved from. Let us look at something very interesting that I find extremely important to understand. When you really pay close attention to Verses 13 and 14 of Chapter 2, compared to what Jesus said in Matthew, it makes you wonder what is really going on.

- Verse 13: *"And suddenly there was with the angel a multitude of the heavenly host praising God and saying:*

- Verse 14: *"Glory to God in the highest, **and on earth peace**, goodwill toward men!"*

Here we have a multitude of heavenly hosts praising God and saying, *"Peace on earth and goodwill toward men"* because the bringer of peace is born, and on top of that we have John the Baptist, who was sent before the bringer of peace to *turn the hearts of the fathers to the children, and the hearts of the children to their fathers.*

Now, Jesus says something very strange in Matthew 10:34-35.

- Verse 34: *"Do not think that I came to bring peace on earth. I did not come to bring peace but a sword."*

- Verse 35: *"For I have come to set a man against his father, and daughter against her mother and a daughter-in-law against her mother-in-law."*

Now that was a huge shift in prophecy! However, as we move through the process, you will understand what's going on.

Let us look at the next key verse that explains what is coming soon. We will be reading from Luke 1:67-79. This is Zacharias, who is filled with the Holy Spirit and begins to prophesy concerning John the Baptist, and the promises that God has promised to the children of Israel. It is very important that you pay close attention to the things that Zacharias is prophesying as it tells us what they are being saved from, and what prophecy proclaimed already.

- Verse 67: *"Now his father Zacharias was filled with the Holy Spirit, and prophesied, saying:*

- Verse 68: *"Blessed is the **Lord God of Israel**, for He has visited and **redeemed His people**."* Verse 69: *"And has raised up a horn of salvation for us in the house of His servant David,*

- Verse 70:*"As He spoke by the mouth of His holy prophets, who have been since the world began."*

- Verse 71:*"That we should be saved from our enemies and from the hand of all who hate us."*

I want all of you to note what was said so far from Verses 67 to 71. Notice that Zacharias is *full of the Holy Spirit* while he is prophesying and saying the Lord *"God of Israel,"* and the redeemed of *"His people."* Notice also that he said God spoke it by the mouth of His holy prophets. It is very important that you notice what Verse 71 says: *"That we should be saved from our enemies and from the hand of all who hate us."*

Well, here we see that Zacharias is prophesying that the prophecies that were prophesied by the mouth of all the prophets are coming to pass and that they will be saved from their enemies (*physical enemies*) and *all* of the people who hate them. Well, we all know that Jesus came teaching them the *opposite* of what Zacharias and prophecy said. Instead of Jesus bringing *peace on earth,* and saving them from their enemies, and from *all* the people who *hate* them, Jesus tells them He did not come to bring *peace,* and that they *would be hated by all people, and thrown into prison and persecuted for His name sake.*

Why the sudden change? What happened to prophecy? As we continue going through the process of prophecy, you will see what happened. Prophecy will be fulfilled and everything that prophecy said will happen. Right now there is a *pause* on prophecy, and we are going to see it as it is happening a little later on.

- Verse 72: *"To perform the **mercy promised to our fathers** and to **remember his holy covenant,***

- Verse 73: *"The oath which He **swore to our father Abraham:***

- Verse 74: *"To grant us that we, being **delivered from the hand of our enemies,** might **serve Him without fear,***

- Verse 75: *"In holiness and righteousness before Him all the days of our life.*

- Verse 76: **"And you, child, will be called the prophet of the highest; for you will go before the face of the Lord to prepare His ways,**

- Verse 77: *"To give knowledge of salvation to his people by the remission of their sins.*

- Verse 78: *"Through the tender mercy of our God, with which the Dayspring from on high has visited us;*

- Verse 79: *"To give light to those who sit in darkness and the shadow of death, to guide our feet into the way of peace."*

Now we have a good understanding about what John the Baptist will be doing before the Messiah, the Christ, the Savior, the bringer of peace, the deliverer, the king of Israel comes.

For twenty-seven to thirty years, there was silence until God told John the Baptist to go and prepare the children of Israel for what they have been waiting for all this time, their land, king, and heavenly ruled kingdom to be a kingdom of priests, and a holy nation to the Lord to bring all the other nations to God. And so it was music to their ears to finally here those words come from John the Baptist's lips, *"Repent, for the **kingdom of heaven is at hand**,"* Matthew 3:2.

Generation after generation, the children of Israel have been waiting for their king, and their heavenly ruled kingdom to come so they could be a kingdom of priests to the world. And so it was good news to finally hear that the kingdom was at hand, and their king the Messiah was on His way to baptize them with the Holy Spirit, which is their promised New Covenant.

In Chapter 3, I gave you the three steps it took for Aaron and his sons to become priests over Israel. For a reminder, those steps are:

1. Wash with water
2. The pouring of the anointing oil on the head
3. Blood on the ear, hand, and foot

The kingdom was at hand and the king was on his way, and John the Baptist was sent before the king to prepare the children of Israel. So what would be the first thing they would have to do? Yes! Be washed with water (baptism).

There are three Greek words for baptism:

1. *Bapto*, which means *to dip*.
2. *Baptizo*, which means *to wash*.
3. *Baptizmos*, which means *a ceremonial washing*.

I know there is a lot of speculation on baptism, so I am going to deal with baptism for a little while and then I will jump back to the process of prophecy.

Some people believe that baptism was something *new* when John the Baptist came, and that no one knew that this baptism was going to happen. That is not so. Baptism, which only means washing was not something new. The children of Israel already knew that they would be a kingdom of priests to the world once the kingdom came. And so once John the Baptist came and told them that the kingdom was at hand, look at what happened in Matthew 3:5-6.

- Verse 5:*"Then **Jerusalem, all Judea,** and **all the region around Jordan** went out to him*

- Verse 6:*"and **were baptized by him** confessing their sins."*

As you can see, everyone went and were baptized by him because they already knew what prophecy proclaimed would happen. Even the Pharisees sent people out to John the Baptist to ask him if he was Elijah, or the Christ, or the prophet that Moses said will come in Deuteronomy

18:15-18. And when John the Baptist said that he is not neither of them, they said to him, *"Why then do you baptize if you are not the Christ, nor Elijah, nor the prophet?"* John 1:25.

All the children of Israel knew that this baptism (washing) would come once Elijah came to prepare the way. This was not something new to them; this was prophecy being fulfilled right before their eyes.

Now, there is a big twist to all of this because we know that John the Baptist was the one who revealed the Messiah to the people, and said, *"Behold the lamb of God."* This same John the Baptist who, while in prison sent his disciples to Jesus to ask Him if He was the one, or do they wait for another (Matthew 11-2-3).

Now why would John the Baptist, who baptized Jesus, and saw the Holy Spirit come down on Him, and said with his own lips, *"behold the lamb of God who takes away the sins of the world,"* ask that question? We will see why later on.

Some people believe that baptism symbolizes Jesus' death, burial and resurrection, but that is not so. Baptism had nothing at all to do with Jesus' death, burial and resurrection.

For one thing, the entire three years of Jesus ministry, all the people that were getting baptized didn't know that Jesus was going to die and rise again on the third day. On top of that, Jerusalem, all Judea and the entire region around Jordan was baptized before they even knew who Jesus was. I know that a lot of people got confused with what the apostle Paul said in Colossians 2:12 and Romans 6:3, and thought that Paul was talking about water baptism when he said we were buried with Christ in baptism, and when he said, as many of us were baptized into Christ Jesus were baptized into His death. Now, I can see how this could be a little confusing, but it is very important you understand that there is only one way to be baptized into Christ Jesus, and believe me it is not by water as that would require someone else to do it for you. If my salvation is dependent upon someone else to baptize me into Christ, God help the world. Well it is not, praise God for that. It is by the Holy Spirit that we are baptized into Christ (1 Corinthians 12:13).There is only one thing that symbolizes Jesus' death, burial and resurrection, and that is the Lord's supper that Jesus said to do in remembrance of Him (Matthew 26:26-28 and 1 Corinthians 11:23-26).

Some people believe that baptism shows that you are a believer in Christ, and that it is an outward expression of an inward conversion. That is not true at all because baptism has nothing at all to do with being a Christian.

Some people believe that Jesus was baptized to be an example because Jesus did not have any sin. This is true, and not true. It is true that Jesus had no sin, but it is not true that Jesus was baptized to be an example. Jesus was not baptized to be an example. He was baptized because *he had to*. Jesus had to be baptized because He was going to be a priest as well, but according to the order of Melchizedek, and because He was under the Law, He *had to fulfill all the righteous requirements*. That was why when John the Baptist tried to prevent Jesus from getting baptized (because Jesus was the one who baptized with the Holy Spirit), Jesus said to John the Baptist, *"Permit it to be so now, for thus it is fitting for us to fulfill all righteousness,"* Matthew 3:15. And as soon as Jesus came up out of the water, **then the Holy**

Spirit came down on Him and the heavens were open and God was well pleased with His obedience to the righteous requirements that God set in order.

Baptism was also a requirement for them to enter into the kingdom of heaven, or kingdom of God, which means the same thing.

In Chapter 2, I gave you three major things that threw people off, and one of them was the combining of the kingdom of heaven with the heavenlies that the apostle Paul said, "*We are already seated in Christ.*"

Many people got confused with what Jesus said in John 3:1-5 and tried to make the water in this verse to mean something other than baptism because of the things that the apostle Paul taught. Now, if you try to bring the apostle Paul into the process of prophecy, you will definitely have to change the water in John 3:1-5 to mean something other than baptism. You will also have to change many things that Jesus, John the Baptist, and Peter said as well.

It is very important that you keep in mind that at the time of John 3:1-5, the apostle Paul is not raised up yet, and the children of Israel has not yet been cast away. And baptism is mandatory for them to enter into the kingdom of God and that is because baptism was for exactly what it said it was for at that time, the remission of sins. I know the apostle Paul's letters are coming to mind right now, but you have to remember once again that Paul has not been raised up yet, and everyone is still under the Law at this time. It is not a misprint what Zacharias said John the Baptist will be doing before the Messiah comes in Luke 1:77:

- Verse 77: *"To give **knowledge** of **salvation** to **His people by the remission of their sins.**"*

- It is not a misprint in the gospel of Mark 1:4:

- Verse 4: *"John came baptizing in the wilderness and preaching a **baptism** of repentance **for the remission of sins.**"*

- Itis not a misprint in the gospel of Luke 3:2-3:

- Verse 2:*"While Anna's and Caiaphas were high priests, **the word of God came to John the son of Zacharias in the wilderness.**

- Verse 3:*"And he went into all the region around the Jordan preaching a **baptism** of repentance **for the remission of sins.**"*

Jesus meant exactly what He said in John 3:5, *"Jesus answered, Most assuredly I say to you, unless one is born of **water** and **the Spirit**, he **cannot enter the kingdom of God.**"*

I will return to John 3:1-5 shortly because it is important to understand, why Jesus uses the term *born of water*, and *born of spirit*, instead of *baptize with water* and *baptize with the spirit.*

It is not a misprint what Jesus said in Mark 16:16:

- Verse 16: *"He who believes **and is baptized** will be saved; but he who does not believe will be condemned."*

- It is not a misprint what Peter said in Acts 2:38:

- Verse 38:*"Then Peter said to them "Repent, and let every one of you be **baptized** in the name of Jesus Christ **for the remission of sins;** and you shall receive the gift of the Holy Spirit."*

It is not a misprint what Ananias told Paul to do in Acts 22:16:

- Verse 16:*"And now why are you waiting? Arise and be **baptized, and wash away your sins** calling on the name of the Lord."*

- It is not a misprint what Peter said in 1Peter 3:18-21:

- Verse 18:*"For Christ also suffered once for sins, the just for the unjust, that He might bring us to God being put to death in the flesh but made alive by the Spirit,*

- Verse 19:*"By whom also He went and preached to the spirits in prison,*

- Verse 20:*"Who formerly were disobedient, when once the Divine long-suffering waited in the days of Noah, while the ark was being prepared, in which a few, that is eight souls, were **saved through water.***

- Verse 21:*"**There is also an antitype which now saves us—baptism (not the removal of the filth of the flesh,** but the answer of a good conscience toward God), through the resurrection of Jesus Christ."*

Yes! You read it right, Peter just said that eight souls were saved *through water,* and that there is an *antitype, which now saves* them, *baptism,* and that it is not to wash away the dirt from their flesh, but the answer of a good conscience toward God. And yes! John the Baptist came preaching a baptism of repentance, and it was definitely for the remission of sins just as the Bible said it was for.

Now, I know that many scriptures are coming to mind right now, especially the *"great commission"* in Matthew 28:19. Well, just hold on, and by the grace of God everything will become clear for you once we make it through the process, and Israel gets cast away, and the apostle Paul is raised up and the mystery of grace takes over.

Now, back to John 3:1-5, as it is very important to understand because this is a ruler of the Jews that Jesus is talking to and Jesus says something very interesting.

- Verse 1: *"There was a man of the **Pharisees** named Nicodemus, a **ruler of the Jews.***

- Verse 2: *"This man came to Jesus by night and said to Him, "Rabbi, we know that You are a teacher come from God; for no one can do these signs that You do unless God is with him."*

- Verse 3: *"Jesus answered and said to him, "Most assuredly, I say to you, unless one is born again, he cannot **see** the kingdom of God."*

I want you to notice that Jesus said, *"Unless one is **born again** he cannot see the kingdom of God.* I believe we all know that God's kingdom is a spiritual kingdom, and cannot be seen with the physical eyes. And the only way to *see* the kingdom of God is for you to be born of the Holy Spirit to *see* it with your spiritual eyes. Throughout scripture, Jesus says, *"He who has ears to hear let him hear."* Now, we all know that everyone had ears and heard him speak, but they did not have spiritual ears so they did not understand. Everyone had eyes, but they did not have spiritual eyes and so they were blind even though they had physical eyes to see.

In Verse 4, we see that Nicodemus was caught off guard and asked a question that he should have already known the answer to, especially when he was a ruler of the Jews, and a teacher of Israel. Jesus just told him what has to be done to *see* the kingdom of God, now Jesus is going to tell him what has to be done to *enter* the kingdom of God.

- Verse 4: *"Nicodemus said to Him, "How can a man be born when he is old? Can he enter a second time into his mother's womb and be born?"*

- Verse 5: *"Jesus answered, "Most assuredly, I say to you, unless one is born of **water** and **the spirit** he cannot **enter** the kingdom of God."*

Now there is a good reason why Jesus uses the term *born of water* and *born of spirit,* instead of using the term that John the Baptist used which was *baptize with water* and *baptize with the spirit.*

In John 1:1, it says, *"In the beginning was the Word, and the Word was with God, and the Word was God."*

Well that same *word* that was in the beginning in the Garden of Eden that said to Adam, *"In the day you eat of the tree of the knowledge of good and evil you will surely **die,**"* is the same *word* that is standing in front of Nicodemus telling him that he must be *born again.* Why? Because Adam ate of the tree and spiritually died, and death reigned through him to everyone born in the world, and Jesus is telling him that he has to be born again spiritually not physically just to see the kingdom of God.

And because the kingdom of heaven was at hand, which was coming down on earth in Jerusalem at that time, and can only be seen by the spiritual things that were happening, the children of Israel had to be water baptized to enter into it. Now, there's a big twist to this as well because Jesus knew that they would not enter into the kingdom at that time, and prophecy was going to be on hold, and that they would be cast away because of the unbelief of the Pharisees and the Scribes that stopped the children of Israel form entering into the kingdom as Jesus said in Matthew 23:13: *"But woe to you, Scribes and Pharisees, hypocrites! For you* **shut up the kingdom of heaven** *against men; for you neither go in yourselves,* **nor do you allow those who are entering to go in."**

As you can see, Jesus was upset with the Scribes and Pharisees throughout Matthew 23 because Jesus wanted to give the kingdom to the children of Israel as He said in Luke 12:32: *"Do not fear, little flock, for it is your Father's good pleasure to give you* **the kingdom."**

Jesus had a big problem with the Pharisees because they were perverse and wicked, and like Jesus said, their father was the devil. But they were Jews as well, and were waiting on the kingdom of God to come even though they were the very ones that stopped the children of Israel from entering the kingdom once it was at hand. Let us read what the Pharisees said to Jesus in Luke 17:20-21.

- Verse 20:*"Now when He was asked by the Pharisees when the kingdom of God would come, He answered them and said, "The kingdom of God does not come with observation;*

- Verse 21:*"Nor will they say, see here! Or see there! **For indeed, the kingdom of god is within you."***

The kingdom of God could not be seen with the human eyes because it was a spiritual kingdom that was coming down on earth in Jerusalem, and you would not be able to say "There it goes right there!" or "Look right their! "But you could see that it was there by the spiritual things that were happening at the time. All of the miracles—people being raised from the dead, Jesus telling the winds to be quiet and they obeyed Him, Jesus feeding thousands of people with only two fish and five loaves of bread, the apostles, and Jesus casting out demons with a word,

Jesus cursing the fig tree and it wither away immediately, and Jesus and Peter walking on the water. These wicked Pharisees were looking to see the kingdom of God come down to earth with their natural eyes, but Jesus told them that the kingdom of God is within you.

Now do not get this wrong, Jesus is not telling these wicked Pharisees that God's kingdom is inside of them. The Greek word for within is **entos**, which comes from the root word **en** and it means *in your midst* or *amongst you*. Remember the kingdom of heaven was close to them, it was at hand to where they could see the effects of it, but not the kingdom itself, and Jesus was telling them that the kingdom of god is around them, in their midst.

Now we can see why Jesus told His twelve apostles to pray *"your kingdom come"* in what people call "The Lord's Prayer" when the apostles asked Jesus to teach them how to pray in Luke 11:2.

Well, this is not "The Lord's Prayer" because Jesus had no sin and Verse 3 could only apply to the twelve apostles who had sin that needed to be forgiven. Theologians misnamed this prayer. It should have been named "The

Apostles Prayer" because they asked Him to teach them how to pray. If you want to know what "The Lord's Prayer" is, you can find it in John 17:1-26. Now keep in mind that Jesus already new that the kingdom of God would be taken from them and given to another just as He said in Matthew 21:43, *"Therefore I say to you, **the kingdom of God** will be **taken from** you and given to a nation bearing the fruits of it."* You also have to keep in mind that even though Jesus knew that Israel would be cast away, which is what most of the parables meant, the process of prophecy had to still move forward while Jesus was on earth.

And so the kingdom was still being offered to the children of Israel if they repent. And they were to still go out and preach the gospel (good news) of the kingdom to the children of Israel, not to the Gentiles because the Gentiles were never waiting for a King or a kingdom to come. Only the Jews were waiting on the king of Jews to come, and the kingdom that He would bring.

We all know by the apostle Paul that Israel was cast away, and did not receive their kingdom because of the wicked Pharisees, but at what point did they get cast away? This is very important to understand to know when Israel's kingdom gospel ended and our grace gospel started. Jesus knew all the answers, and what was going to happen, and told them to their faces, in parables so that they would not understand it, we will look at one of the parables to see the time frame, and then I'll get back to the process of prophecy.

This is a parable that most people spiritualize to make it fit them, but we are going to get the proper understanding of the parable. Turn with me to Luke 13:6-9.

- Verse 6: *"He also spoke this parable: "A certain man had a fig tree planted in his vineyard, and he came seeking fruit on it and found none."*

- Verse 7: *"Then he said to the keeper of his vineyard, 'Look for three years I have come seeking fruit on this fig tree and find none. Cut it down; why does it use up the ground?"*

- Verse 8: *"But he answered and said to him, 'Sir, let it alone this year also, until I dig around it and fertilize it.'"*

- Verse 9:*"And if it bears fruit, well. But if not, after that you can cut it down."*

This is the interpretation of the parable. The *certain man* is *Jesus,* and the *fig tree* is *the children of Israel,* and the *vineyard* is *Jerusalem.* And the *keeper of the vineyard* is *God.* The certain man(Jesus) came looking for fruit on the fig tree (Israel), and found none. Then he (Jesus) said to the keeper of his vineyard (God) *"Look for three years I have come seeking fruit on this fig tree (Israel) and found none. Cut it down; why does it use up the ground?"*

Remember, Jesus started His ministry at age thirty, and died on the cross at age thirty-three. Jesus came to His own, the children of Israel for three years trying to get fruit from them, but they weren't bearing good fruit, so Jesus said to God (keeper of the vineyard),

"Cut it down; why does it use up the ground?" Remember the last prophet Malachi said in Chapter 4, Verse 1 that He will leave them neither root nor branch. And John the Baptist said in Matthew 3:10 to the children of Israel that even now the ax is laid to the root of the trees. And that the tree that does not bear good fruit is cut down. Well,

the keeper of the vineyard (God) said, *"Sir, let it alone this year also, **until I dig around it and fertilize it**. And if it bears fruit, well. But if not, after that you can cut it down."* Now, the period of the *"Let it alone this year also, until I dig around it and fertilize it"* is the Acts period.

In Acts, Peter tried to get them to repent, but they did not listen and threw him in prison. Then Stephen, who was full of the Holy Spirit, gave them the longest sermon in Acts 7:1-60, trying to tell them the same thing, but they still did not listen. Instead, they covered their ears, ran at him and stoned him to death. And so they were cut off just like John the Baptist said would happen if they did not bare good fruit because the ax was already laid at the roots of the tree. Just as Jesus said in the parable, *"Cut it down; why does it use up the ground?"* that is exactly what happened. They were cut off(cast away), *and we were grafted in*. We will be going through this process as well to get a better understanding of what happened when they were cast away, as we continue going through the process of prophecy.

Right now, I am going to repeat the three steps it took

for them to become priests, because I am going to use Jesus as a quick example so that you can have a general idea of what is going on when we make it back to the process of prophecy. This is needed as many changes are going to take place. It is very important that you keep in mind that Jesus already knew that Israel was going to be cast away from the time He started His ministry.

The three steps are once again;
1. Wash with water.
2. The pouring of the anointing oil on the head.
3. Blood on the ear, hand, and foot.

Okay, if Jesus is going to be a priest as well, what is the first thing that Jesus would have to do? Yes! Be washed with water. And so Jesus was baptized by John the Baptist.

Now, what would be the next step that Jesus would have to do? Yes! Pour the anointing oil on the head. And so Jesus was anointed with the Holy Spirit as it was poured out from heaven on Jesus as soon as he came up from the water. (The Holy Spirit represents the anointing oil in the Old Testament.) Now, what is the last thing that Jesus would have to do? Yes! <u>Blood on the</u> ear, hand and foot. And so

Jesus took care of that on the cross as He was nailed in the hands and foot, and a crown of thorns was pressed into his head. This was the picture of what Aaron and his sons were doing with the blood in the Old Testament. Always remember that everything in the Old Testament pointed to Jesus Christ. Every story that you read is a picture of Jesus.

- Abraham offering up his only son is a picture of God offering up His only son.

- Joseph being hated by his brothers for no reason is a picture of Jesus being hated by His own people for no reason.

- Joseph being sold for pieces of silver is a picture of Jesus being sold for pieces of silver.

- Joseph being lied on by his master's wife is a picture of Jesus being lied on by the Jews.

- Joseph being thrown into prison because of the lie is a picture of Jesus being taken into custody because of the lies.

- Joseph was in prison with two men that were working for the Pharaoh, and they both had a dream, and Joseph told one of them that he would be restored back to the Pharaoh in three days, and the other one that he would be hanged on a tree and die. This is the picture of Jesus on the cross with the two thieves on both sides, and one of them was restored as he asked Jesus to remember him when He come into His kingdom, and the other one died in his sins.

- Joseph coming out of prison and being made ruler over everything is the picture of Jesus rising from the dead and being made ruler over everything in heaven and in earth.

All the pictures in the Bible are so powerful and perfect, that it blows me away every time I read them.

Chapter 4

Back to the process of prophecy. Right after Jesus was baptized, and the Holy Spirit came down on Him, He was led to the wilderness to be tempted by the devil. I really want to explain why He was led to the wilderness to be tempted, but it would take us off track because there would be too many details that I would have to explain. However, I do believe that it is important that I bring up the three things that Jesus was tempted with, because these three temptations are the same temptations that were used in the beginning of time, and moved into Jesus' time, and also what we are being tempted with every day.

Hebrews 4:12 says that Jesus was tempted in all the points that we are tempted. And we all know what those three temptations are:
1. The lust of the flesh
2. The lust of the eye
3. The pride of life

And yes! It started back in the Garden of Eden when the serpent said to the woman, *"You would not surely die."* Then Genesis 3:6 says, *"So when the women saw that the tree was good for food **(the lust of the flesh)** that it was pleasant to the eyes **(the lust of the eye)**, and a tree desirable to make one wise **(the pride of life)**, she took of its fruit and ate."*

These are the same three temptations that Jesus was tempted with in Luke 4:1-15, when the Devil told Jesus to turn the stone into bread (lust of the flesh). Then the Devil showed Jesus all the kingdoms and said that he would give them to Jesus if He would fall down and worship him(lust of the eye).Then the Devil told Jesus to jump off the pinnacle of the temple if He is the son of God because the angels would save Him(pride of life).

After the temptations, Jesus started His ministry. I want to take you to the gospel of Matthew 4:17 because it shows the first thing that Jesus taught the people: *"From that time Jesus began to preach and to say,* **"Repent, for the kingdom of heaven is at hand."**

Well, we all know now whom Jesus is talking to. He is telling the special people above all other people on the face of the earth(The Jews) that the kingdom is at hand, and to repent because they were in sin.

By Verse 22, Jesus picks a couple of disciples. And in Verse 23, we can see what gospel (***good news***) Jesus is preaching.

Let us read it together:

- Verse 22: *"And Jesus went about all Galilee, teaching in their synagogues, preaching "the gospel" (good news) of the kingdom, and healing all kinds of sickness and all kinds of disease among the people."*

Then in Chapter 5, Jesus starts teaching the multitudes of people on the mountain. In Verses 11 and 12, Jesus starts speaking in terms of the future events that will come after He dies, because Jesus already knew that they were going to reject Him as their king, and the people that believed in Him.

Then in Verse 13, Jesus deals with prophecy, and tells the children of Israel that they are the salt of the earth, because they are the ones that were supposed to bring the rest of mankind to God. He also tells them that if the salt loses its flavor, how then can it be seasoned? It would be good for nothing, but to be thrown out and trampled underfoot by men. In other words, if the special people above all other people on the face of the earth (the Jews) lose their position of being the example to the world, they would be good for nothing because God chose them to be a kingdom of priests to the world, and a holy nation to bring the rest of the world to God.

In Isaiah 60:1-22, we can see what was going to happen to the children of Israel once the Christ comes. Let us read a little part of the prophecy.

- Verse 1: *"Arise, shine;* **for your light** *has come! And the glory of the Lord* **is risen upon you.**"

- Verse 2: *"For behold, the darkness shall cover the earth, and a deep darkness the people; but the LORD will arise* **over you** *and* **his glory will be seen upon you.**"

- Verse 3: *"The Gentiles shall come to your light, and kings to the brightness of your rising."*

So in Matthew 5:14, Jesus continues with what prophecy says, and tells *the children of Israel*(the special people above all other people on the face of the earth) that *they are the light of the world,* and that a city that is set on a hill cannot be hidden.

For those who do not know, the city on the hill is Jerusalem. And yes! It really sits on the top of a hill. By Verse 16, Jesus tells the children of Israel to let their light shine so that men will see their good works and glorify their Father in heaven. And throughout Chapters 5 and 6, Jesus teaches the children of Israel how to act so that they could be an example to the rest of the world to bring everyone else to God. Well we all know that they were not a good example, and killed their king, and later was cast away, but while prophecy is unfolding let us keep our minds focused on what is going on.

Now, let us turn to the gospel of Luke 4:16, when Jesus came to Nazareth where He had been brought up because when Jesus goes into the temple and reads from the book of the Prophet Isaiah, something very strange happens while He's reading.

This is the first place that we will see the pause on prophecy that Jesus already knew would be coming soon. It starts in Luke 4:16-21.

- Verse 16: *"So He came to Nazareth, where He had been brought up. And as His custom was, He went into the synagogue on the Sabbath day, and stood up to read."*

- Verse 17: *"And He was handed the book of the Prophet Isaiah. And when He had opened the book, He found the place where it was written:*

- Verse 18: *"The Spirit of the LORD is upon Me, Because He has anointed Me to preach the gospel to the poor; He has sent Me to heal the brokenhearted, To proclaim liberty to the captives And recovery of sight to the blind, To set at liberty those who are oppressed;*

- Verse 19: *"To proclaim the acceptable year of the Lord."*

- Verse 20: *"Then He closed the book, and gave it back to the attendant and sat down,* **and the eyes of all who were in the synagogue were fixed on Him."**

Why were all the people in the synagogue staring at Jesus? The reason is: Jesus left out the biggest part of the prophecy. Let's see what that was that He left out which caused everyone to stare at Him, expecting Him to finish the verse. Jesus quoted from Isaiah 61:1-2.

- Verse 1: *"The Spirit of the Lord God is upon Me, Because the Lord has anointed me to preach good tidings to the poor; He has sent Me to heal the brokenhearted To proclaim liberty to the captives, And the opening of the prison to those who are bound;*

- Verse 2: *"To proclaim the acceptable year of the LORD,* **and the day of vengeance of our god."**

Well, as you can see, Jesus left out **"and the day of vengeance of our god,"** and closed the book and sat down. And so everyone's eyes in the synagogue were fixed on Him.

Then the part that Jesus quoted, He tells them that it is fulfilled today in their hearing.

Now this is very important to understand because John the Baptist told them when they came to his baptism, *"Who warned you to flee from the wrath to come?"* That is because the last days started with John the Baptist, and the day of vengeance, which is God's wrath, was supposed to come in their time, according to prophecy. Even the apostles were saying that the time was close. And even Peter told them that they are in the last days, as he quoted the Prophet Joel in Acts 2:16-21. So what happened? The wrath of God, which is the day of vengeance, did not come and here we are around two thousand years later, and the wrath of god still has not come. Why is that?

Well, I can tell you that Jesus did not leave out the part, *"and the day of vengeance of our God,"* of His reading of Isaiah the Prophet for nothing, and as we go on we will see why He left it out.

Let us take this time to look at a couple of places where we can see the pause on prophecy, and then we will jump back to the process of prophecy.

In Acts 2, the day of Pentecost came and the promise of the Holy Spirit came down on the apostles in the upper room. When the people heard the apostles speaking in their own language from where they were born, they were shocked and thought that they were drunk.

When Peter heard what they said, he stood up and told the people that they were not drunk as they supposed, but that this was the fulfillment of the prophet Joel, and then Peter quoted what the prophet said.

We are going to read Acts 2:16-21 together because this is extremely important to understand because Peter is saying that this prophecy is being fulfilled, right before their eyes.

- Verse 16:*"**But this is** what was spoken by the prophet Joel:*

- Verse 17: *"And it shall come to pass in the **last days**, says God, that I will pour out of My Spirit on all flesh; Your sons and your daughters shall prophesy, your young men shall see visions, your old men shall dream dreams."*

- Verse 18: *"And on My menservants and on My maidservant I will pour out My spirit in those days; And they shall prophesy."*

- Verse 19: ***"I will show wonders in heaven above and signs in the earth beneath: blood and fire and vapor of smoke."***

- Verse 20: *"**The sun shall be turned into darkness, and the moon into blood,** before the coming of the great and awesome day of the Lord."*

- Verse 21: *"And it shall come to pass that whoever calls on the name of the Lord shall be saved."*

Well, we all know that the top part of the prophecy was fulfilled because the Holy Spirit was poured out on them just as prophecy said, but what about the bottom part of the prophecy? If this prophecy is being fulfilled in their time like Peter said, then that means Verses 19 through 21 should have happened as well because it is all one prophecy. So what happened?

Well, guess what? Just as Jesus read from the book of the Prophet Isaiah and closed the book right when He came to the part (and the day of vengeance of our God) because He knew that there was going to be a pause on prophecy, well, this is the same thing that is going on here. The pause happened right between Verses 18 and 19.

Now everything that was said in Verse 19 was the same thing that Jesus was telling His apostles in Luke 21:25-26.

- Verse 25: *"And there will be **signs in the sun, in the moon,** and in the stars; **and on the earth distress of nations,** with perplexity, the sea and the waves roaring;*

- Verse 26: *"Men's hearts failing them from fear and the expectation of those things **which are coming on the earth,** for the powers of **the heavens will be shaken."***

We also can see it in Matthew 24:29, *"immediately after the tribulation of those days **the sun will be darkened,** and **the moon will not give its light;** the stars will fall from heaven, and the **powers of the heavens will be shaken."***

Then we see the same thing is told to John after Jesus died and rose from the dead in Revelation 6:12-17:

- Verse 12: *"I looked when He opened the sixth seal, and behold, **there was a great earthquake;** and **the sun became black as sackcloth of hair,** and **the moon became like blood.***

- Verse 13: *"and the **stars of heaven fell to the earth,** as a fig tree drops its late figs when it is shaken by a mighty wind.*

- Verse 14: *"then the **sky receded as a scroll when it is rolled up and every mountain and island was moved out of its place.***

- Verse 15: *"And the kings of the earth, the great men, the rich men, the commanders, the mighty men, every slave and every free man, hid themselves in the caves and in the rocks of the mountains,*

- Verse 16: *"and said to the mountains and rocks, "fall on us and hide us from the face of him who sits on the throne and from **the wrath of the lamb!***

- Verse 17: *"for the **great day of his wrath has come**, and who is able to stand?"*

Now there is a big twist to all of this as well, because if you read Chapter 7:18, you will notice there is one hundred and forty-four thousand people that are going to be sealed during this time. And guess what? They are from the twelve tribes of Israel, and he even names the twelve tribes that will be sealed at that time. Well, I am not from any of the twelve tribes of Israel so what about the Gentiles? What happens to us at this time?

Well, I can tell you this; you are going to be blown away when we get to the part of what happens to us who are saved right now, during that time.

Okay, let us look at one more place where we can see the pause on prophecy. Now, this one is very powerful and blows me away every time I think about it. I want you to pay close attention to everything that is said and shown because this shows us where we are right now as it relates to prophecy. I know that we have a lot of people and theologians who are trying to calculate the times that we are in by using prophecy and Israel as the time clock, and wondering why they keep coming up short of their calculation. Well, the reason is that God's time clock stopped the moment Israel was cast away. Take a look for yourself.

Exodus — 4th year of Solomon's Reign = [480 years]
1 Kings 6:1

According to Paul, Wilderness wandering [40] years Acts 13:18

+ Period of judges [450] years Acts 13:20

+ Saul's Reign [40] years Acts 13:21

+David's Reign [40] years 1 Kings 2:11

+ Solomon's first 3 years [3] years

= [573 years] TOTAL.

Paul records a time period of [93 years] longer than what is stated in 1 KINGS 6:1. Why is that?

Why is Paul *off* by [93 years]?

Well, let us find out why. In the book of Judges, there are *five* periods of servitude that is recorded.

First servitude —   [8 years] [Judges 3:8]

Second servitude — [18 years] [Judges 3:14]

Third servitude — [20 years] [Judges 4:3]

Fourth servitude — [7 years] [Judges 6:1]

Fifth servitude — [40 years] [Judges 13:1]

= [93 years] TOTAL.

Well, as you can see, Israel's years of servitude equal the difference between Paul's and Solomon's account, and that is because the lord's prophetic calendar takes no notice of periods when Israel is in bondage [lo-ammi] (cast away). Paul, however, was using the world's calendar in which these time periods are included. Israel has been [lo-ammi] (cast away) status since Acts 28:28. And so prophecy stopped, and there is this mystery period that we are in right now, and the apostle Paul was raised up to proclaim it.

I do not want to jump into the mystery period right now, but I am going to because of what was just said. I want you to see what the apostle Paul had to say about this mystery period that we are in right now. Let us turn to Romans 11:25-29.

- Verse 25: *"For I do not desire, brethren, that **you should be ignorant of this mystery,** lest you should be wise in your own opinion, **that blindness** in part has happened* *to Israel **until** the fullness of the **gentiles has come in.**"*

I want you to notice that Paul is telling us Gentiles that he does not want us to be ignorant of this mystery (secret), that Israel was blinded just for a time, and that it is not permanent, but just until the fullness of the Gentiles has come in. After he finished saying that, he quotes prophecy in Verses 26 and 27 to show us that prophecy still has to be fulfilled.

- Verse 26: *"And so **all Israel will be saved,** as it is **written:** "the deliverer will come out of Zion, and he **will turn** away ungodliness from Jacob;*

- Verse 27: *"For this is **my covenant with them,** when I take away their sins."*

As you can see, Paul is telling us that God made a covenant with the children of Israel that has to be kept, and that God will keep His word.

Then the apostle Paul gives us a clearer understanding of what is going on with the gospel that he preaches to us Gentiles in Verses 28 and 29, and how it relates to Israel at this time of the mystery period.

- Verse 28: *"Concerning **the gospel** **they are enemies** for your sake, but concerning **the election** they are **beloved for the sake of the fathers**.*

- Verse 29: *"For the gifts and the calling of God are irrevocable."*

The apostle Paul is telling us that the children of Israel are enemies of "the gospel" that he preaches, and that it is for our sake, but they are beloved because of the sake of the fathers, and because God made a covenant that He cannot break.

I will deal with more of the apostle Paul's letters as we move from the process of prophecy to the mystery period of grace because people have misinterpreted the apostle Paul's letters and came up with us being spiritual Israel, which caused them to spiritualize everything in the Bible.

Okay, let us get back to the process of prophecy.

Chapter 5

I am going to continue with the process of prophecy by pointing out John the Baptist and the question he sent his disciples to ask Jesus.

Most people have thought that John the Baptist doubted that Jesus was the Christ, but that is not true at all. Others have thought that he asked the question for his disciples to know the answer, but that is not so. He asked that question for a real good reason.

Now keep in mind that we are going through the process of prophecy, that the apostle Paul has not been raised up yet, everybody is still under the Law at this time, and no one is under grace yet, and that there is a big difference between Jews and Gentiles.

Also, keep in mind that no one has the apostle Paul's letters or any book of the Bible from Matthew up to Revelation. The only thing that the people had was the Old Testament, which includes the Law, the Prophets, the Psalms, and the Torah, which is the first five books of Moses.

Now, as we all know, God told John the Baptist to go and baptize the people, and that the one who he sees the Spirit descending, and remaining on, is the one that baptizes with the Holy Spirit (John 1: 33).

So of course, John the Baptist saw the Spirit come down on Jesus and remained on Him. Therefore, John the Baptist bore witness that this is the one, and said that this is the son of God (John 1:34).

John the Baptist also said in John 1:29,*"Behold! The Lamb of God who takes away the sin of the world!"* On top of that, John the Baptist said that *"This is the one that I was talking about who shoes I'm not worthy to lose."* Then John the Baptist said that he must decrease so that Jesus could increase (John 3:30). So we all know for a fact that John the Baptist knew for sure that Jesus was the Christ, the son of God. So why did he ask Jesus if He the coming one or do they wait for another? Well, the reason is because John the Baptist knew the scriptures and what prophecy said would happen. And for John the Baptist to witness seeing the Christ without Elijah, who was supposed to prepare his way, John the Baptist was confused on prophecy, not that he doubted. He said that he was not Elijah, but little did he know that he was actually playing the role of Elijah.

That is why the angel told Zacharias that John the Baptist would go in the spirit of Elijah. And that is why John the Baptist was filled with the Holy Spirit from his mother's womb. And that is also why Jesus said that John the Baptist was more than a prophet, and that there is not one born of woman who is greater than John the Baptist.

However, the twist to all of this was the hidden prophecy of Jesus' death, burial and resurrection that had to be fulfilled.

And so in John 12:27-34, Jesus tells them that the Son of Man must be lifted up from the earth, and the people responded with what prophecy said about the Christ and what would happen when the Christ comes in Verse 34:

"The people answered Him, "We have heard from the Law that the Christ remains forever and how can you say, the Son of Man must be lifted up? Who is this Son of Man?"

Notice that everyone is confused with everything that Jesus was saying, but they knew that when the Christ comes that He would restore Jerusalem back to Israel and sit on the throne of David and remain forever.

That is why the people were telling Jesus, when He was on the cross, that if He is the Christ to save Himself from death and come down from the cross because, according to prophecy, the Christ was going to come and gather the lost sheep of Israel, rule as king, sit on the throne of David, and restore Jerusalem back to Israel.

That is why all the people doubted that Jesus was the Christ because Jesus did not save Himself from death. And Jesus later on, after he rose from the dead, He opened the scriptures to His disciples about His death, burial and resurrection (Luke 24:44-49).

All the Jews knew the scriptures and the prophecies, but no one new that Jesus was going to die and rise on the third day because that part was hidden in the scriptures and had to be revealed after He rose from the dead.

Now, I want you to notice Jesus' response to the question that John the Baptist asked Jesus (Luke 7:18-23).

- Verse 22: *"Jesus answered and said to them, "Go and tell John the things you have seen and heard: that the blind see the lame walk the lepers are cleansed, the deaf hear, the dead are raised, the poor have the gospel preached to them."*

- Verse 23: *"And blessed is he who is not offended because of Me."*

I want you to notice that Jesus did not say, "Tell John yes, I am the Christ." But Jesus told them to tell John the Baptist what they heard and saw which was all the things that prophecy said the Messiah would be doing when He comes.

I also want you to notice what Jesus said in Verse 23 that *"Blessed is he who is not offended because of Me."*

The Greek word for *offend* is *skandalizo*, and it means *to put a snare or stumbling block in the way*. So, in other words,

Jesus is saying, *"Blessed is he who is not stumbling because of Me."*

Jesus knew that everyone was going to stumble at the shift in prophecy and what He came to do. And because Jesus knew the hidden prophecy concerning Himself, He told His apostles that they were going to be made to stumble in Matthew 26:31.

The apostle Peter, who knew that Jesus was the Christ, felt that he was not going to stumble because the Christ will fix all the problems according to prophecy. And so Peter said that if everybody else stumbles, that he is not going to stumble. But once again the hidden prophecy is what Peter was missing and so Jesus told peter that He will deny Him three times.

But guess what? John the Baptist was not the only one that was confused when it came to prophecy. The twelve apostles were confused as well because when they came down from the mount of transfiguration in Matthew 17:10, they asked Jesus, *"Why do the scribes say that Elijah must come first?"*

Well, Jesus knew that prophecy still had to be fulfilled and that when Elijah came that He would restore all things just like prophecy said would happen. So in Verse 11, Jesus confirms prophecy and tells them that Elijah is coming first and that He will restore all things because prophecy said it will happen.

Then Jesus goes on to say in Verse 12, concerning His mission and the hidden prophecy that would later be revealed, which is His death, burial and resurrection, that Elijah has come already and they did not know him, but did to him whatever they wished. Jesus goes on to say that He is going to suffer at their hands as well. In Verse 13, the disciples understood that Jesus was talking about John the Baptist.

It is very important that we understand that when Elijah comes according to prophecy that he will restore all things. And if Jesus also came to fulfill hidden prophecy and die on the cross, then the real Elijah could not have come the first time because everything would have been restored like prophecy said and Jesus would not have died.

Now because of the hidden prophecy that had to be fulfilled, we had John the Baptist come in the spirit of Elijah so that the Christ could die and fulfill the hidden prophecy.

And so now when the real Elijah comes, prophecy will be fulfilled because he will restore all things and Jerusalem will be restored back to Israel for the thousand-year reign, and Jesus will come and sit on the throne of David just like prophecy said He would do.

Now because of the hidden prophecy and Jesus omniscient ability Jesus talked to the Jews in parables so that they would not understand Him (Matthew 13:10-17).

And all the parables in Matthew, Mark, Luke, and John are dealing with the Jews the Law, hidden prophecy, and things concerning the topic that was at hand at the time, as well as future events.

I know that we have spiritualized the parables to fit our situations, but all the parables that Jesus told the children of Israel were for a reason.

Let us take the parable of the prodigal son in Luke 15:11-24, for instance. We have taken the prodigal son parable and spiritualized it to fit a backsliding Christian.

But the parable has its own interpretation. The prodigal son is the unbelieving Jew (sinner) that was given the Law, but he left and started living a sinful life, and the son that got angry that the father threw a party for the prodigal son are the Pharisees and Scribes.

To understand the prodigal son parable fully you would have to start at Luke 15:1.

- Verse 1: *"Then all the **tax collectors** and **the sinners** drew near to Him to hear Him."*

- Verse 2: *"And the **Pharisees and Scribes** complained, saying, "This Man **receives sinners** and eats with them."*

- Verse 3: ***"So he spoke this parable to them saying:"***

I want you to notice the first parable that Jesus told them after the Pharisees and Scribes made that statement because Jesus uses three parables back to back because of their statement. Jesus starts with the parable of the lost sheep, and going after the lost sheep in Verses 4 through 7, which was a part of His mission.

And please keep in mind that the lost sheep does not have anything at all to do with the gentiles, but only the children of Israel and what prophecy said about the lost sheep.

Do not worry I will get to us gentiles when we move from Israel's kingdom gospel to the grace gospel.

Then Jesus speaks another parable using the lost coin dealing with the same statement in Verses 8 through 10 with the same thought in mind relating to the sinning Jews who are still sons of the kingdom but are lost, and the Pharisees and scribes who are Jews, and sons of the kingdom as well.

Then we see in Verses 11 through 24 that Jesus continues the same train of thought and uses another parable to say the same thing, but in the analogy of two sons.

The Pharisees and Scribes had a problem with Jesus because he was hanging around sinners (backsliding Jews). But the Pharisees and Scribes didn't know that Jesus came for them because they were the lost sheep of Israel.

Jesus got on the Scribes and Pharisees' cases, but in parables, they were mad that Jesus was healing, forgiving, and saving the sinners.

Therefore, it is very important that we have the right understanding of the parables so that we do not build doctrine on speculation.

Most of the parables that I want to explain would have to wait until we move from the process of prophecy into the grace period. This is because for us to understand most of the parables, especially those dealing with future events, you would have to have a good understanding of the difference of what Jesus taught the Jews while they were under the Law, from the things that the apostle Paul taught when grace took over, and they went from being under the Law to being under grace.

There is so much that I want to touch on that relates to the process of prophecy, but most of it will lead us in different directions that would have to be explained in full detail to fully understand what's going on.

And because I know that it would take us too far off track because of all the changes that takes place and has to be explained as it happens, I'm going to just deal with the process of prophecy that will lead us straight into the grace period.

I want to deal with one more part of Matthew and Luke that will shine some light on some of the things that Jesus was saying in relation to the kingdom gospel, and the transition that was coming.

Now keep in mind that Jesus already knew what was going to happen to the children of Israel, and that the kingdom that was at hand that they were supposed to enter was going to be taken away from them.

And Jesus knew what was going to happen once the kingdom that was at hand was taken away.

And so He spoke about it in a way that they could not understand, but we can now understand it in our time because we have the whole picture.

Let us turn to Matthew 12:43-45 where we are going to read it together.

- Verse 43: *"When an unclean spirit goes out of a man, he goes through dry places, seeking rest, and finds none.*

- Verse 44: *"Then he says, 'I will return to my house from which I came. 'And when he comes, he finds it empty, swept, and put in order.*

- Verse 45: *"Then he goes and takes with him seven other spirits more wicked than himself, and they enter and dwell there; and the last state of that man is worse than the first. So shall it also be with this wicked generation."*

Now what is Jesus talking about here? What is the use of casting out a demon that could return and bring seven more wicked ones with him? What is the use of raising Lazarus from the dead just for him to die again? What is the use of healing someone from a disease just to die from something else? What is the use of the twelve apostles having the power to heal the sick and raise the dead, when all of the people they healed and raised from the dead died again? What is the use of the apostles having the power to raise the dead when they all died themselves?

I want you to keep these questions in the front of your mind because all the answers are locked in Israel's kingdom gospel.

I want you to notice that Jesus said, *"So shall it be with this wicked generation,"* speaking of the generation that He was born in.

I also want you to notice that Jesus said throughout the four gospels that the generation was a wicked, perverse, evil, and adulterous generation (Matthew 12:39, Matthew 16:4 and Luke 11:29).

So now we have to keep the right context of the scripture when the apostle Peter said that they are a chosen generation and a royal priesthood (1 Peter 2:9).

So what is Jesus telling the people in Verses 43 through 45 about the unclean spirit that brings more wicked ones with him? Well, Jesus was telling them something that was coming soon.

Jesus already knew that God's spiritual kingdom that was coming down on earth in Jerusalem at that time would not fully come down because of the wicked Pharisees and scribes that stopped it from coming when it was close, or at hand.

And once the kingdom that was at hand was taken away from them like Jesus said was going to happen, then the demons are going to come right back and bring even more with them.

Remember Jesus said that His kingdom was not from this world and if it was from this world that his servants would fight so that He would not be delivered to death(John 18-36).

Well, this world is Satan's kingdom and everything in it. That is why Satan was able to offer it to Jesus when Jesus was being tempted.

This earth is a physical earth, but Satan and his demons control it. That is why the apostle Paul said that we are *in* this world but we are not *of* this world, and to be transformed by the renewing of our minds. So if Jesus who is the king was coming to rule and bring His kingdom with Him as well, then that means that Satan and his demons have to go.

So Jesus gave the apostles and the seventy the power to cast them out and get rid of them. And so they were being cast out because the kingdom of God was at hand, and coming down on earth which means Satan's kingdom was being taken from him. The big twist to all of this is Jesus knew already that the children of Israel were not going to accept Him as their king on earth at that time, or the kingdom that was at hand.

And Jesus also knew that the children of Israel were going to get cast away, and that the kingdom of God was going to be taken away from them. Which means all of those demons that were being cast out, was going to come right back and bring even more with them, and it was going to happen in the time frame of that wicked generation just like Jesus said.

I am going to take you all a little deeper into this topic just in case I may have confused some of you a little bit.

Okay, Jesus brought up the topic of the unclean spirit going right back to where they started from and bringing even more wicked ones with him in Verses 43 through 45 because of what was said in Verses 22 through 30. We are going to read it together so that we can get a good understanding of what Jesus is saying.

- Verse 22: *"Then one was brought to Him who was demon-possessed, blind and mute; and He healed him, so that the blind and mute man both spoke and saw.*

- Verse 23: *"And all the multitudes were amazed and said, "could this be the Son of David?"*

- Verse 24: *"Now when the Pharisees heard it they said, **"This fellow does not cast out demons except by Beelzebub, the ruler of the demons.***

- Verse 25: *"But Jesus knew their thoughts, and said to them: "Every kingdom divided against itself is brought to desolation, and every city or house divided against itself will not stand.*

- Verse 26: *"If Satan casts out Satan, he is divided against himself.* **How then will his kingdom stand?**

- Verse 27: *"And If I cast out demons by Beelzebub,* **by whom do your sons cast them out?** *Therefore they shall be your judges.*

- Verse 28: "But if I cast out demons by the *Spirit of God,* **surely the kingdom of God has come upon you.**

- Verse 29: *"Or how can one enter a strong man's house and plunder his goods, unless he first* **binds the strong man?** *And then he will plunder his house.*

- Verse 30: *"He who is not with Me is against me, and he who does not gather with Me scatters abroad."*

Okay, in Verses 22 and 23 we see that Jesus cast out a demon and everyone was amazed, and said, *"Could this be the Son of David?"* Then in Verse 24, we have the Pharisees that said Jesus only casted out the demons by Beelzebub the ruler of the demons. Then, of course, Jesus knew their thoughts and said to them in Verse 25 that *"Every kingdom that is divided against itself is brought to desolation, and that every city, or house that is divided against itself will not stand."*

Then Jesus goes on to say in Verse 26 that *"If Satan cast out Satan, he is divided against himself. How then will **his kingdom stand?**"*

Of course Satan's kingdom is right here on earth, and if he were casting himself out then his kingdom would not stand.

Then Jesus goes on to say in Verse 27 that *"If He cast out demons by Beelzebub, **by who do their sons cast them out?** And that they would be their judges."*

For those who do not know the sons that Jesus is talking about, here are the seventy that Jesus sent out two by two who came back happy that the demons had to listen to them (Luke 10:17).

And so Jesus tells them in Verse 28 that *"If He cast out demons by the spirit of God that surly the kingdom of God has come upon them."*

And in Verse 29, the strong man is Satan, and Verse 30 is self-explanatory.

Well we all know that Jesus was casting out the demons by the spirit of God because God's kingdom was coming down upon them at that time.

We also know that the children of Israel denied their king, got cast away, and did not enter the kingdom that was at hand because it was taken away from them which means those demons that were cast out came right back once God's kingdom was taken back up, and wasn't at hand anymore.

The most important thing to know and fully understand is the time frame dealing with the transition from Israel's kingdom gospel to the grace gospel.

Because understanding the time of the transition and when it took place will also shine some light on the understanding of why the miracles, healings, opening the eyes of blind people, and raising the dead are not being done in our time, as it was when the kingdom of god was at hand.

Now please do not get me wrong, God can do whatever He wants at any time because He's God and all powerful, but all of the miracles, healing's, and raising the dead was for a reason, and it all had to do with Israel's kingdom gospel and the fulfillment of prophecy. We will deal with this topic of miracles, raising the dead and healings as we move into the Acts period. We are also going to deal with some of the scriptures that people have been misinterpreting for a long time. I'm going to make some statements that will shock you at first, but will become clear and evident as we move through the process. Everything I say will be backed up with scripture, and if it is not backed up with scripture then this book, and the up-coming ones is false doctrine and you are to get rid of them.

In the beginning of the upcoming book, the first thing we will look at is what people thought was the great commission in Matthew 28:19.

- Verse 19: *"Go therefore and make disciples of all the nations, baptizing them in the name of the Father and of the Son and of the Holy Spirit,*

- Verse 20: *"Teaching them to observe all things that I have commanded you; and lo, I am with you always, even to the end of the age."*

People have thought that this was the great commission, but guess what? It is not.

We are going to see that it's not together as we go through the process. Now, do not get me wrong, this is a commission to go and preach "the gospel," but it was not the grace gospel that the apostle Paul preached. It was Israel's kingdom gospel that they were commission to go and preach.

Keep in mind that Israel is not cast away at this time, and they were commission to go and make disciples of all the nations and baptize them.

Now the part that confused everyone is when Jesus said, *"All the nations."* Well, we will get the right understanding of "all the nations" part as we go through the process and see it for ourselves. And we will get a better understanding of all the other misinterpreted scriptures that we have thought was explained correctly.

May the Lord prepare your heart and mind for part two.

www.ingramcontent.com/pod-product-compliance
Lightning Source LLC
Chambersburg PA
CBHW071405290426
44108CB00014B/1686